The Private Lives
of
Eva & Adolf

The Private Lives
of
Eva & Adolf

Adapted from *Eva* and *Adolf*

by Glenn B. Infield

Grosset & Dunlap

A Filmways Company

Publishers   New York

Adapted from *Eva* and *Adolf*

Photographs from the National Archives

Contents

1. The Young Eva

*As a young girl Eva Braun sought adventure
and excitement. She found both in the person of
Adolf Hitler.*

When Eva Braun was born in 1912, Adolf Hitler was twenty-three years old. He was living in Vienna, painting scenes to be reproduced on postcards to earn money for food. Eighteen years after Eva was born, however, she would "take a bath, put on her best underclothes" and leave her home in Munich to meet the man who would later become Führer of Germany and the most infamous despot of modern times.

Eva growing up; this was taken shortly before she started working for Heinrich Hoffmann, Hitler's official photographer.

Fritz Braun, a schoolteacher, and his wife were highly respected middle-class citizens of pre-World War I Munich. They were the parents of a three-year-old daughter and devout Catholics who attended mass every week. His neighbors considered Fritz Braun's morals impeccable. Though he liked his beer, he never flirted with other women—in fact, his male friends at the local *bierhaus* considered him something of a prude because he objected to their lewd stories and obscene jokes.

Franziska Katharina Kranbürger Braun, known to everyone in the neighborhood as Fanny, was the most beautiful woman in the northeast section of Munich. Twenty-seven years old, with a slender waist, shapely legs and full breasts, she had more than enough appeal to keep her husband from straying. She was also a very athletic young woman, especially adept at swimming and skiing. Many who knew the couple wondered why this beautiful Dresden doll was so devoted to the gruff, rough-featured Fritz; but devoted she was, and their family life was happy.

When his wife became pregnant the second time Fritz Braun was confident that she would bear a son. He loved his three-year-old daughter Ilse but he wanted a son to carry on the Braun name. There was no doubt in his mind on the cold evening of February 6, 1912, that soon he would have one. As midnight approached, his mother-in-law, who had come to Munich from her home in the province of Oberpfalz to oversee the birth of the baby, looked at the nervous Fritz and nodded. "It won't be long now."

At twenty-five minutes past two on the morning of February 7, 1912, the baby was born—a girl. After his initial disappointment that the child was not a boy—a disappointment that disappeared as soon as he looked at the small bundle his mother-in-law allowed him to hold—Fritz Braun tried to think of a name for the new arrival. He had selected a name for the son he expected—Rudolf, in honor of Crown Prince Rudolf of Austria who had been found slain in his hunting lodge near Vienna in 1889. Fritz had always admired and respected the Crown Prince even though when he was murdered the Baroness Maria Vetsera had been with him. Now that it was obvious Rudolf could not be used, he decided after

considerable thought to name the baby Eva Anna Paula. He completely forgot that European custom meant her birthday would be celebrated on her patron saint's day, and since Saint Genevieva's Day was one day before Christmas, his new daughter's birthday and Christmas presents would be combined. In later years Adolf Hitler would always take advantage of this custom.

Eva was a healthy baby who soon had father, mother and three-year-old sister busy keeping her out of trouble. She was a pink-cheeked, robust child who laughed often and, as was the German custom, enjoyed the privileges of being the "baby" of the family. Even her father's stern warnings seldom kept her out of mischief until he had emptied his next stein of beer. Ilse spent a great deal of time watching her younger sister for her mother, and the two girls became very close. When Eva was three years old another child was born to Fanny Braun—a girl who was named Gretl. This time Fritz Braun was not around to comfort his wife during the birth or to show his disappointment that he still had no son. He was in the German Army.

On June 28, 1914, Gavrilo Princip, an Austro-Hungarian student, shot and killed Archduke Franz Ferdinand of Austria and his wife in the Bosnian capital of Sarajevo. Fritz Braun immediately recognized the seriousness of the assassination. He was aware of the antagonism between Austria–Hungary and Serbia, caused by the territorial demands of Serbia, and knew that while the assassin was of Austro–Hungarian nationality, he was a Serbian by

Eva, age two (right) with friends.

birth. Consequently, Fritz Braun was not surprised when Austria–Hungary declared war on Serbia on July 28, 1914, an action that resulted in World War I and eventually set the stage for Adolf Hitler's political career.

Eva was too young to understand where her father had gone when he joined the German Army. She missed him. She adored the father whose harsh words and occasional slaps on the behind couldn't hide his affection for her. For several weeks after he left for Flanders, Eva was so quiet and subdued that her mother was convinced she was ill. The old doctor who examined Eva just shook his head, however, and said he couldn't find anything physically wrong with the girl. "I think she misses her father," he told Fanny Braun. "She is young. She will soon get over it and be as lively as ever."

It was an accurate diagnosis. Eva was soon running around the house and laughing as she had before her father left for the army. It was fortunate that her energy and activity were restored to their usual level, because they were needed. It was a difficult time for Fanny Braun and her three daughters. From the beginning of the conflict Germany was handicapped because her food, manpower and raw materials were more limited than those of the Allies, and her citizens were forced to make sacrifices that had not been anticipated. Germany had not prepared detailed plans for the management of her wartime economy and paid the price for this neglect. She was unable to maintain her agricultural production at the prewar level because the military drained a large segment of manpower and horses from the villages and farms, and fertilizer became scarce when nitrogen—one of its components—was diverted to the manufacture of explosives.

While Fanny Braun did not know the details of such military and agricultural problems, she did know they seriously affected her and her three small daughters. Meat, butter, potatoes and other foods were in short supply, and she had to hunt daily to find enough to eat. One winter she and the girls lived primarily on turnips, since other foods were available only on the black market and Fanny didn't have the money to buy them. It has been estimated that about three-quarters of a million Germans died of hunger that winter, but Fanny Braun and her small brood survived. She made army uniforms and other items that brought in a small amount of money, and she took in lodgers. By being very frugal Fanny and the girls managed to eat and keep warm during the four years Fritz Braun was gone.

Eva, who was six years old when her father returned home from the war, had changed very little in disposition despite

the hardships. She remained a fun-loving, mischievous child and was the one bright spot in the life of the Braun family during the miserable years immediately following World War I. Inflation in postwar Germany wiped out everyone's savings and insurance policies, and government bonds were not worth the paper they were printed on. Though Fritz Braun resumed his teaching career, his salary was inadequate to maintain his wife and three daughters in prewar comfort. Deprived of their sense of security, he and thousands of middle-class citizens like him felt betrayed by the government and deeply resented the immoderate demands of the triumphant Allies at Versailles. It was against this background of economic breakdown and bitterness that the numerous political parties of the country jockeyed for power. One of these parties was the National Socialist German Workers' Party (NSDAP), led by Adolf Hitler. Fritz Braun refused to have anything to do with the Nazi organization, whose leader he considered a "jack-of-all-trades, an imbecile who thinks himself omniscient and who wants to reform the world."

Eva was too young and too busy enjoying life to be concerned about political parties or the men who led them. In 1925, when she was thirteen years old, her father inherited a modest sum of money from a distant aunt and the fortunes of the Braun family took an immediate upswing. They moved to a new apartment, much larger and more modern, at 93 Hohenzollernstrasse, about six blocks north of where Eva was born. From their new home Eva and her two sisters often walked west a few blocks, cut north on Tengstrasse and went into Luit-pold Park to play. If they tired of that park they went an equal distance in the opposite direction to the huge, famous Englischer Garten (English Gardens), which had a lake, horseback riding areas and several playgrounds. Eva was quick to follow in her athletic mother's path and soon became an excellent swimmer and ice skater. In the winter she learned to ski in the mountains south of Munich, where the family often went on long weekends. Both her parents were proud of her athletic achievements, but Fanny Braun wanted her daughters to learn more than how to do the Australian crawl in the water or a figure-eight on the ice. She recognized that Eva was going to be a problem as far as formal education was concerned. "She has a graceful figure, holds herself well and has a fine disposition," she told her husband, "but she is too frivolous to study hard in school. She will only learn as long as she is being amused."

Fanny Braun's analysis of her daughter's attitude toward school was confirmed when her teacher, Fräulein von Heidenaber, told her that Eva was "intelligent but spends much of her time in class being a troub-lemaker."

Actually, Eva's attitude was influenced by her times. The cultural decline that fol-lowed defeat in the war, the rampant inflation and unemployment, the severe re-strictions put on Germany by the victorious Allies, the political confusion as the various German officials struggled for power, and the prevailing defeatist attitude affected her whole generation. To a young, impression-able girl it seemed best to "live today be-cause tomorrow may never come." Why study the music of Johannes Brahms or Richard Wagner when American jazz tunes were much better for dancing? The writings of Ernst Monism, Wilhelm Dilthey, Fried-rich Nietzche and Thomas Mann did not interest Eva nearly so much as the *Tales of Oscar Wilde* and the Wild West novels of Karl May. Consequently, by the time she was fifteen years old, Eva had the primary and secondary education expected of a girl her age, but had made no effort to delve into the classics of either literature or music. All she wanted was to have a good time, enjoying herself to the fullest and learning only those facts of life that would enable her to do so.

Yet her Catholic upbringing and her father's stern discipline did have some ef-fect on Eva. When Carl Anson, a school-mate, offered her a cigarette, Eva refused to smoke it. She didn't accept a cigarette until a year later when several of her girl friends gathered in the English Gardens one eve-ning and dared each other to smoke. Eva would never back down on a dare, and be-sides, she had wanted to smoke ever since Anson had offered her a cigarette the year before. Unfortunately her first cigarette made her sick, and when she returned home, pale and holding her stomach, her mother gave her a spoonful of castor oil and put her to bed. But the foul-tasting medicine didn't discourage her, and she was a constant smoker for the remainder of

Eva appearing as Al Jolson, one of her favorite American singers; she loved to sing and dance.

Right: Eva loved animals; and she eventually persuaded Hitler to give her a dog which she called Stasi.

Right: Eva, still a young schoolgirl, shows signs of becoming a beautiful woman.

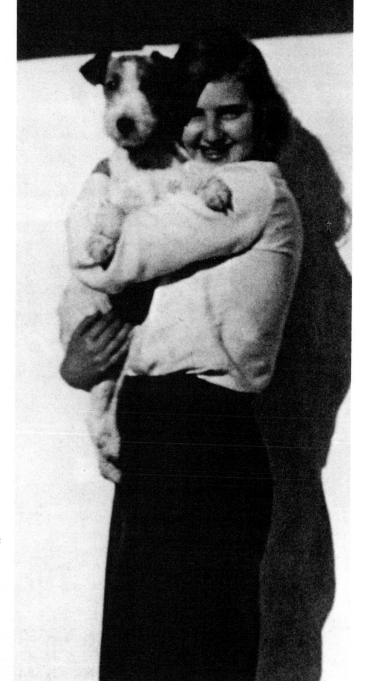

her life . . . even against the wishes of Adolf Hitler.

At fifteen Eva naturally became interested in boys, which infuriated her father. He occasionally permitted her to invite a boy to the Braun apartment while he and Fanny were present, but when Eva asked to go dancing or to a movie with a boyfriend he usually refused even to answer her. Her mother understood her much better, and because of her intervention Eva now and then managed to go out for a few hours with a schoolmate or a neighborhood boy whose reputation Fanny had thoroughly checked. It soon become evident to both her mother and father that the fun-loving Eva could not be kept in the apartment all the time, nor could one of them accompany her every time she stepped outside, so they made a decision. They sent her to a convent school.

Fanny Braun was convinced that a convent school would give Eva the education and social graces required of a real lady. It was then considered prestigious for a young woman to say she had been educated in a *Kloster*, and Fanny was ambitious for her vivacious daughter. She hoped that Eva would become a well-known dressmaker, or better, marry a man whose money and social status would lift her above the humdrum life of an ordinary married woman burdened with children and bills. She wanted her daughter to travel, to meet people in other walks of life who were successful and well known, to achieve the prestige that she herself had never had except in her own intimate circle. It was an ambitious objective, but she was

sure it could be accomplished if Eva were guided correctly during her early years.

In the small town of Simbach, approximately sixty miles east of Munich, the English Sisters—a Catholic order founded by a fugitive from English persecutions—operated a school for young girls. It was there that Eva Braun was sent at the age of sixteen. Simbach was directly across the Inn River from the Austrian town of Braunau, which was gaining fame as the birthplace of the political upstart Adolf Hitler. Eva found the rigors of the Catholic Young Women's Institute difficult to accept, despite the fact that her family was Catholic and strict. Sister Marie-Magdalene took a special liking to her, though, and helped ease her into the disciplined routine of the school. Before long Eva was going to confession twice a week as required, attending all other religious services without protest and adhering to the rules and regulations of the convent. She wasn't happy, however.

"I will never stay here two years," she told Nina Garnier, a classmate, less than a month after she entered the convent. "This is not the life for me."

The one activity at the school that Eva found congenial was the amateur theatricals that were staged periodically. Eva had always been interested in acting, although her only previous experience consisted of studying her favorite actor, John Gilbert, on the screen. At the convent she was permitted to take part in the productions, al-

Even at the so-called awkward age, Eva had an appealing, demure smile.

though she was never a "star"—only a supporting actress. She was an excellent dancer—probably the best among the student body—but there was not much opportunity for a dancer in a convent. Once she was caught putting on a private dancing exhibition for a group of girls when they were all supposed to be in their rooms studying, and she was given a month's restriction to the convent area for her disobedience. She didn't complain, nor did she attempt to put any of the blame on the others.

"I asked them to watch me," she told the Mother Superior, "because I have just learned a new dance. It is my fault."

Eva found the repetitive, dull routine of convent school life unbearable and—instead of subduing her as her parents had hoped—the year she spent there only strengthened her resolve to live a more exciting life. Smoking a cigarette, dancing on the sly and acting in a few amateur theatricals did not fulfill her craving for adventure, and when she finally took her leave of the school in the fall of 1929, Eva was determined that her future was going to be very different.

All her exciting plans faded when she reached the Braun apartment in Munich. Fritz Braun was unhappy that his daughter had left the convent school a year early and displeased with the report he had received from the faculty. It stated, in part: "Your daughter is intelligent and ambitious. She

regularly attended the religious services. Yet she was not interested in the curriculum and thought that the regulations were unduly restrictive."

Her father was intelligent, too, and he realized that the sisters were politely telling him that Eva was too rambunctious for the convent, that her ideas and the ideas of the English Sisters were entirely different. He decided to take immediate steps to bring his daughter into line. He checked on every letter Eva received and every telephone call she made or received at the apartment. She had to be in her room at ten o'clock every night, and just to make certain that she didn't read the books or magazines that might not meet his approval, he shut off the electricity in her room at that hour. Eva managed to read anyway by using a flashlight and hiding under the blankets. It was an austere life for a seventeen-year-old girl, one that was designed to break her of what her father considered to be frivolous habits. Instead it made her more determined than ever to find an exciting life outside the Braun apartment.

Lack of money finally gave Eva the excuse she needed to get away from the family circle. Despite Fritz Braun's inheritance and his promotion to full professorship at the school where he was teaching, he couldn't afford to give Eva any personal spending money. Once in a while her mother managed to slip her a few *pfennigs* from her household money, but not often. Eva decided to look for a job. When she first suggested the idea to her father he just shook his head, but after thinking it over he reconsidered. He had read about the severe depression in the United States and knew that if history repeated itself Germany's economy would feel the effects of the American depression within a year. Therefore he decided that it would be a good idea if his daughter did bring in some money to help with the family bills. Eva, of course, was not thinking of the Braun family debts. She was planning on using the money for clothes, jewelry, cosmetics and other personal items.

While her father had been concentrating on reshaping her outlook toward life, Eva had been concentrating on revamping her physical appearance. When she returned from the convent school she noticed that her sister Ilse, three years her senior, was using cosmetics. Ilse, who was working as a receptionist for a doctor, knew that her appearance was of vital importance. She watched her weight, bought clothes that were in fashion and made herself up to look more attractive. At first Eva thought that applying lipstick, powder, and eyebrow pencil was a waste of time, but when she started looking for a job she soon discovered just how important her appearance was to prospective employers—especially if they were male. Little by little she learned the art of makeup, studied fashions to determine which styles were best for her and spent many hours arranging and rearranging her hair. She decided that she was too heavy, although she was only a little on the plump side and was considered ideal for a German girl of her age. She went on a diet, but—knowing her father would consider it a "foolhardy girlish stunt"—pretended that she had an upset stomach so he wouldn't force her to eat. Eva complained about her "upset stomach" so often that her mother sent her to a doctor, who couldn't find anything wrong with her. When Eva told him the truth the doctor sided with her and told Fritz Braun that it would be best if his daughter limited her food intake because of a "nervous stomach."

After three months of dieting and experimenting with clothes and makeup, Eva had changed from the round-faced, pigtailed school girl of the English Sisters' convent into a fashionable young woman. She lacked the stylish clothes she wanted so much and her mannerisms were still more giddy than sedate, but all her acquaintances noticed the difference. When Hilda May, a neighbor girl who lived on Kaiserstrasse, teased her about her cosmetics, Eva had an answer ready. "If a few *pfennigs* of cosmetics will get me what I want," she said, "it is money well spent."

Now she began to learn about a more sophisticated life from another of her acquaintances, Klara Oster, a beautiful dark-haired girl who worked as a secretary at the offices of the Industry Club in the Park Hotel in Düsseldorf. While Klara was home on vacation Eva met her walking in the English Gardens, and they spent the afternoon together. Klara explained that in her position she often met wealthy and influential industrialists and, with a laugh, told Eva that sometimes they would give her expensive gifts.

"Why?" Eva wanted to know. "Are you an excellent typist?"

At first Klara thought Eva was teasing her, but when she discovered her friend

was serious she explained a few facts of life to her.

"I *am* an excellent typist, but so are hundreds of other girls in Düsseldorf. No, they don't give me gifts because of my typing. They do it because I am nice to them. I go to dinner with them when they are lonely, laugh at their jokes and try to keep them in good humor as much as possible." Seeing the shocked look on Eva's face, Klara smiled. "Now don't get any wrong ideas, Eva. I don't go too far."

Later that evening, when Eva told her older sister Ilse about her conversation with Klara Oster, Ilse warned her that it was a dangerous game Klara was playing—but one that was often effective. This was a lesson Eva Braun would remember when she

lent photographer who had apprenticed under his father and uncle, both of whom had photographed many members of royalty. After his apprenticeship he joined Hugo Thiele, court photographer to the Grand Duke von Hessen in Darmstadt, for a period, moved on to Heidelberg the next year to work with Langbein, the university photographer, and in 1902 was in Frankfurt taking pictures of military officers for the Theobald Studio. Later Hoffmann worked in London, where he also began publishing art books. By 1910 he was back in Germany and opened a studio of his own in Munich. Within a few years Hoffmann had established himself as one of the best photographers in the city and was a moderately wealthy man. He was also supremely confident. When he was offered a fee of one hundred dollars to provide a picture of the radical politician Adolf Hitler to an American agency in 1922 he thought it would be just another easy assignment.

Hoffmann, who had joined the Nazi Party two years earlier because he approved of its platform for the recovery of Germany, did not know Hitler when he accepted the assignment. When he approached him about the photograph he discovered that Hitler had a fetish about having his picture taken. He believed an important factor in his hypnotic hold on an audience was the fact that they had never seen a photograph of him. Surely, Hoffmann insisted, Hitler was no better than the emperors, kings,

was introduced to Adolf Hitler.

Shortly after Klara returned to Düsseldorf Eva answered an advertisement in the *Munchener Neueste Nachrichten* concerning a position at a photography shop at 50 Schellingstrasse. The owner of the shop was a short, heavy-set Bavarian named Heinrich Hoffmann, a vulgar man who loved drinking and women equally. He was an excel-

Heinrich Hoffmann's studio in Munich where he introduced Adolf Hitler, as Herr Wolf, to Eva.

Right: Eva with Heinrich Hoffmann, the only man permitted by Hitler to take his picture.

queens and other famous people who had permitted him to photograph them? His pleas were completely ignored and he didn't get the photograph. He did, however, become good friends with Hitler during the next two years, and Hitler spent many hours relaxing at the Hoffmann home. It wasn't until 1924, when Hitler was released from the prison at Landsberg, that Hoffmann got permission to take his picture. From then on he was known as "Hitler's photographer." At the time the title didn't signify much, but later it brought

Hoffmann worldwide fame and wealth.

When Eva entered his shop late in 1929, Hoffmann was delighted with her pretty appearance and her youthfulness. He liked young girls, not only for personal reasons but also because they were good for business. He hired her immediately to work as a clerk, part-time bookkeeper and assistant in the darkroom developing film. Later Hoffmann proposed another duty for young Eva, one that was to change her life. He asked her to entertain his friend Hitler.

At approximately the same time that Heinrich Hoffmann hired Eva, Adolf Hitler rented a luxurious nine-room apartment in a fashionable section of Munich several blocks southeast of the photography shop. He wanted a more appropriate place to invite his associates and friends.

2. The Meeting

In 1929 Hitler moved into a large, plush apartment on Prinzregentenstrasse, one of Munich's most fashionable streets, bought a new and expensive wardrobe, acquired a fleet of modern automobiles and hired twelve people to take care of his living quarters and belongings.

One of the frequent visitors to Hitler's new apartment on Prinzregentenstrasse was Heinrich Hoffmann. Hoffmann was undoubtedly the best-known photographer in Munich in 1929. His close association with Hitler and the Nazi Party had earned him large sums of money and prestige, but this was not his only source of revenue. He periodically published illustrated books such as *A Year of Revolution in Bavaria*, which brought him a gross profit of half a million. marks. He was also in demand from wealthy and socially conscious Germans who wanted their photographs taken by "Hitler's photographer." By 1929 he had branch studios in Berlin, Vienna, Frankfurt, Paris and The Hague and employed more than a hundred persons. His wife, who had been a great help to him, died during the flu epidemic that swept Munich in 1928, and by the time Eva Braun applied for a job at his Schellingstrasse studio he desperately needed an assistant. Not so desperately, however, that he didn't appraise the young girl for more than mere ability to handle a clerking job. Hoffmann considered himself an expert judge of feminine beauty, and most of his female employees had been selected as much for their appearance as for their work habits and abilities. He was at-

Eva, taken in 1929, shortly before she met Hitler.

tracted to the young, naïve Eva immediately. In some ways she reminded him of his daughter Henriette, who, he discovered later, was only three days older than Eva. He hired Eva at a small salary and she went to work in his studio the following day.

Eva was delighted with her new position. Her commercial studies at the Catholic Young Women's Institute qualified her for bookkeeping chores, but within a few weeks she was doing a variety of tasks for Hoffmann. She clerked, inventoried stock, ran errands and even learned how to develop film. She enjoyed this work in the darkroom more than any of her other assignments and became very proficient at it. During the remainder of her life she was an avid amateur photographer and always developed her own pictures. Since she worked long hours in the studio, usually in close proximity to Hoffmann, she soon learned about politics and the struggle that was in progress in Bavaria and Germany for control of the government. She noticed the attention Hoffmann paid to certain of his clients when they appeared at the studio to have their photographs taken, but she thought it was because they were wealthy and their business added to his already substantial bank account. She learned later, however, that Hoffmann was so attentive because they were associates of Adolf Hitler, one of the politicians trying to gain control of Bavaria. The names Rosenberg, Hess, Bormann, Himmler and Goebbels meant nothing to her; neither did the name Adolf Hitler. Politics was not one of Eva's interests in 1929.

Hoffmann, on the other hand, was vitally interested in Hitler. He was well aware that most of the success he had enjoyed during the past few years was the direct result of his close association with Hitler, and he didn't want that association to deteriorate. He was convinced that Hitler's political platform would eventually lead him to power in Bavaria; when his friend reached that pinnacle Hoffmann wanted to be at his side. Consequently, he plotted every move in his progressing friendship with Hitler as carefully as Hitler himself plotted his political path to power. Hoffmann made certain that every photograph he showed to Hitler was flattering; the negatives of unflattering pictures were destroyed before they left the studio. He would travel across Germany at a moment's notice on an assignment if Hitler requested it. If Hitler was in Munich, Hoffmann made certain that he went to the Café Heck, Hitler's favorite restaurant at the time, to have lunch with him. He knew the more often he was included in Hitler's intimate circle, the more influence he would have. There was one other duty he performed for Hitler from time to time, a duty Hitler never directly requested but appreciated nevertheless. Hoffmann kept a list of attractive women whom he could introduce to his friend whenever Hitler was lonely or bored or both.

There had been a lull in this particular activity ever since Geli Raubal, Hitler's niece, had moved into Hitler's apartment,

Eva's father, Fritz Braun (left), her mother Franziska (second from right), Eva looking over her shoulder.

so the rotund photographer was mildly surprised when he noticed Hitler staring at his new employee one day several weeks after she started to work in his studio. Hitler was an infrequent visitor to the studio in the latter part of 1929 because he was engrossed in politics, and it took Hoffmann a minute or two to realize that this was the first time he had seen Eva. The timing could not have been better as far as Hoffmann was concerned, because he felt that Hitler's interest in him had waned recently and he needed something to reawaken his friend's appreciation of his worth. A new woman would be an ideal contribution.

Eva was standing near the top of a ladder getting a box of film from one of the high shelves when Hitler first noticed her. Hoffmann watched his eyes slowly move up her slim legs, appraise her rounded but firm hips, and finally center on her neatly brushed hair. He could tell that Hitler was eager to see her face so he called to her.

"Come down, Eva. I want you to run an errand."

She looked back over her shoulder at Hoffmann and the man standing beside him and smiled at them both. Hoffmann saw immediately that Hitler was delighted with Eva's appearance. He watched her come down the ladder, but as soon as she touched the floor and headed toward them, Hitler pretended to be busy looking at some photographs on the counter.

"Run across the street and get us some *Leberkaes* and beer," Hoffmann told Eva, handing her a few marks. "Herr Wolf enjoys a second breakfast about this time in the morning."

Leberkaes was a Bavarian sausage that Hoffmann loved. He knew that Hitler wouldn't eat the sausage or drink the beer, since he didn't like either, but he wanted an excuse to introduce the girl to him. Hitler, ever conscious of his image, would resent associating in public with a "mere clerk" unless he had a logical excuse to do so. The sausages and beer provided a legitimate reason for him to join Eva and Hoffmann at a small table in the back of the studio where he could become acquainted with the young girl at his leisure.

"*Ja.*" Eva looked at Hitler, smiled and turned away.

Hoffmann was disappointed. He had anticipated that Eva would be overjoyed to see the celebrated Hitler; when she didn't even change expression it puzzled him. He finally decided that she was confused because he had called Hitler by the pseudonym "Herr Wolf," which Hitler often used in Munich during this period because the Bavarian government had restricted his actions. The photographer didn't understand that the man he idolized meant nothing to Eva Braun.

When she returned a few minutes later with the beer and sausages, Hoffmann invited her to join Hitler and himself at the small table. Eva took the chair next to Hitler and accepted a small glass of beer and two of the sausages. Hitler tried to hold a casual conversation with her but he sounded stiff and formal. As usual, he was unable to engage in light banter with anyone, male or female. Fortunately, Eva could and did. With unusual tact for a girl her age, she quickly realized that the "old man" sitting beside her was attempting to be friendly but didn't know how to go about it, so she took over. At that moment she had no real interest in the stranger except that he was a client of her employer, and what was good for her employer was indirectly good for her. She told Hitler about an incident that had occurred earlier in the morning when she had been trying to get another box of film down from one of the high shelves and had accidently knocked it off the shelf. It had fallen on Hoffmann's cat which, frightened, scurried toward the main door, reaching the entrance just as a bakery clerk carrying bread for Hoffmann entered. The cat knocked the feet out from under the boy who promptly fell headlong into a display of camera tripods. The way she described the scene made the usually sober-faced Hitler laugh, and the tension was broken. Hoffmann encouraged her to tell more stories, and by the time the sausages and beer had disappeared they were all laughing and enjoying their conversation. Hitler relaxed as he and Eva talked about a play at the Staatstheater, about music they both enjoyed and American movies.

After Hitler left the studio Hoffmann called Eva aside and asked, "Do you know that man?"

"Herr Wolf? All I know is that he is a friend of yours, Herr Hoffmann."

The photographer smiled and shook his head. "His name is not really Herr Wolf. That is Adolf Hitler!"

Once again Hoffmann was disappointed. Eva gave no indication that she was impressed.

"Who is Adolf Hitler?" she asked.

Hoffmann was mystified that anyone in Munich—or in all of Bavaria for that matter—could be ignorant of the importance of Adolf Hitler. He just shook his head and walked away. The young girl watched him go and frowned. She couldn't understand why he was so upset with her.

Hitler was indeed well known in Bavaria in 1929. The number of dues-paying members of the Nazi Party had reached 180,000 and was increasing rapidly. Besides the party members who spread the name of Adolf Hitler across the country into every small village, Dr. Joseph Goebbels had been appointed Minister of Propaganda in 1928 for the express purpose of publicizing Hitler's name. He was an excellent choice. The son of a factory foreman and a blacksmith's daughter, Goebbels was born in the town of Rheudt in 1897, eight years after Hitler. Rejected for military service in World War I because of a deformed foot, he attended eight famous German universities, finally taking his Ph.D. degree in 1921 from Heidelberg. A year after his graduation from Heidelberg he heard Adolf Hitler speak at a rally in Munich and promptly joined the Nazi Party. His great gift for public speaking was a talent he used to good advantage for himself and Hitler from that date until his death.

Despite the growing importance of the Nazi Party and the excellent propaganda efforts of Goebbels, Eva was unimpressed by Hitler when they first met. She thought his

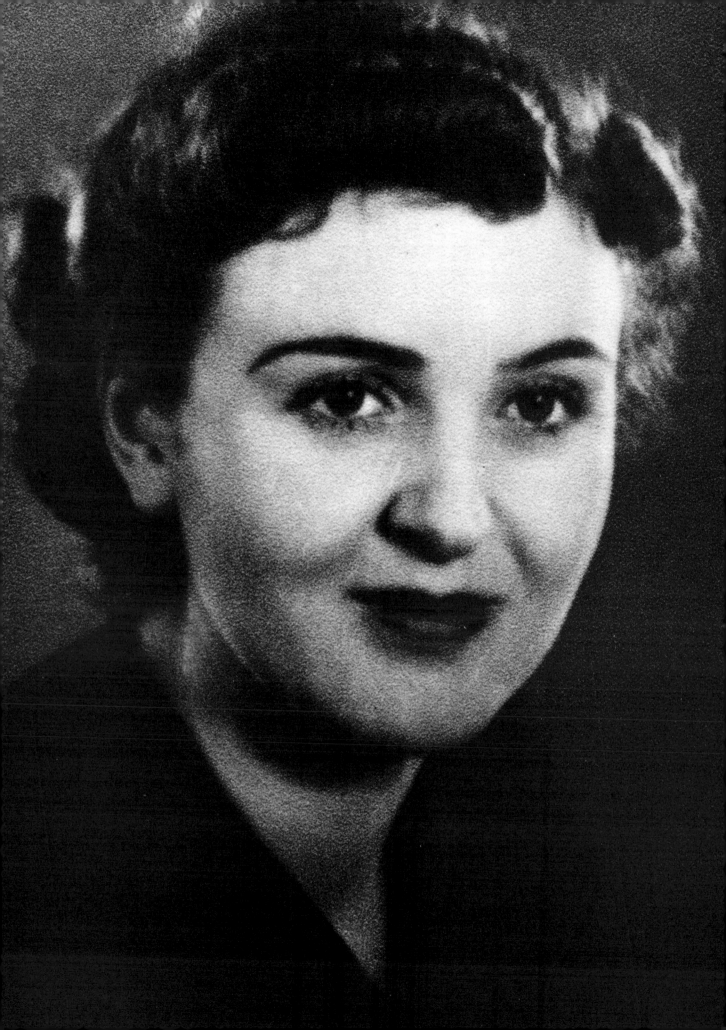

Above & right: Two photos of Hitler's plush apartment on Prinzregentenstrasse into which he moved in 1929.

Left: A more mature Eva—probably taken in the 1930s.

slouch hat and small mustache made him appear comical, and she was critical of the fit of his suit. The collar of the jacket extended out from the back of his neck nearly an inch, and she compared him to a "turtle sticking its head out of its shell." Yet she couldn't forget the look in his eyes when he stared at her in the studio. It wasn't the color (they were a deep blue) but the hypnotic quality that fascinated her. Hitler's eyes had the same effect on many others; even enemies had capitulated when they met him because of his strangely effective eyes. Eva still had not forgotten his stare when she reached the Braun apartment that evening.

"Vati," she asked Fritz Braun that night at the dinner table, "who is Adolf Hitler?"

That was the wrong question to ask in the Braun household in 1929. Fritz Braun considered Hitler a fanatic and was opposed to most of his political program. Fanny Braun's father, who often visited the Braun apartment in Munich, was violently opposed to the Nazi doctrines, and he had convinced Fritz that of all the politicians on the Bavarian scene in 1929, Adolf Hitler was the worst. A personal matter made Eva's father dislike Hitler and the Nazi Party even more. He had been proposed for promotion to assistant master of the technical school where he taught, but when the school officials learned that he was not a member of the Nazi Party they refused to recommend him for the advancement. Fritz Braun had always disliked politics, and after this rebuff he was really disgusted. So when Eva innocently mentioned Hitler's name at the dinner table that evening, her father was furious.

"Hitler? I would not walk on the same side of the street with him. He is a fanatic!"

Realizing the question had made her father angry, Eva dropped the subject immediately and began talking about other matters with her mother. But her curiosity was aroused and she decided to learn more about the man with the "slouch hat and little mustache." The following day, instead of going to a nearby café for lunch, she stayed in the studio and studied the photograph file on Adolf Hitler. Hoffmann had the largest picture collection of Hitler in existence, mainly because he was the official photographer and had an exclusive franchise to sell Hitler's pictures to outside sources. Eva was fascinated by the file of photographs. Some of the pictures showed women trying to break through guard lines to touch him, throwing flowers in his path, reaching for him as he passed in his Mercedes-Benz. There were photographs of him at the theater and the opera with glamorous actresses and fashionably dressed older women who were obviously wealthy and influential. In some of the photographs Hitler had exchanged his slouch hat for a top hat; in others he wore a uniform and brightly polished boots. By the time her lunch hour was over and she had finished examining the file, Eva had revised her opinion of Hitler. She realized now that he was much more than a slightly comical "old man" who enjoyed talking with young girls. He was a celebrity. She hoped he would come to the studio again.

Hitler was extremely busy in 1929, however, and his visits to Hoffmann's were rare. By this time firmly established in Bavarian politics, he had his first opportu-

Hitler examining photographs with Heinrich Hoffman (left, next to Eva), the Führer's official photographer.

nity to break into the national scene and become well known throughout Germany. Because he opposed the action of German Chancellor Gustav Stresemann—Stresemann had agreed to the Allies' renegotiated reparation demands known as the Young Plan, named for banker Owen D. Young, chairman of the Allied committee—Hitler made his name known to millions of Germans who had never paid any attention to him before. His speeches were printed in all the important newspapers of the country and carried over most of the radio stations. Among those most adamantly opposed to the Young Plan were the owners of German heavy industry, and they were pleased with the way the radical

Adolf Hitler had agitated their enemies. They decided to back him financially if he would cooperate with them, and in 1929 Hitler needed the money for his Nazi Party badly enough to agree to their terms. He knew that once he was in power he could do exactly as he pleased without worrying about any promises he had made to the industrialists.

Eva saw very little of Hitler during this period. She had inquired discreetly about his age and discovered that he was forty years old, which, in her seventeen-year-old mind, made him an "old man." The young men who came into Hoffmann's studio and flirted with her were much more lively and able to offer her the fun she was always seeking. Yet she couldn't forget "Herr Wolf."

Shortly after the Reichstag approved the signing of the Young Plan despite Hitler's opposition, Hitler reappeared at the studio.

"Is Herr Hoffmann in the back?"

Eva, who had not seen him enter the studio, looked up directly into his eyes, and for a moment she was confused. After she summoned the photographer from the darkroom, Hoffmann and Hitler went into a back room of the studio and she returned to her task of taking inventory of the items stored under the counter. Both men emerged from the room an hour later. Hitler bowed slightly in her direction and walked out the front entrance to the Mercedes-Benz waiting for him. Hoffmann watched him drive away and then joined Eva at the counter.

"**I** would like to have you come to my house tonight, Eva," he said. "Hitler is going to stop by and he asked that you come too."

That evening at Hoffmann's house in the Schnorrstrasse was the first of many for Hitler and Eva. Hoffmann's home was one of Hitler's favorite hideways during this period of his life, a place where he could find the type of relaxation and repose he sought. With Eva at his side that first evening, he prowled through the house examining the medals and diplomas that Hoffmann had earned during his career. There was the gold medal awarded him by the South German Photographic Association, the King Gustav of Sweden gold medal, the Great Silver Medal of Bugra and many others, all of which impressed young Eva. Since Hoffmann had once been determined to be a great painter, he had a large number of books dealing with art. Hitler, who had also wanted to paint, was fascinated by them.

"At one time I was a pupil in Professor Heinrich Knirr's Academy," Hoffmann explained to them. "Unfortunately, my father had other ideas and insisted that I should adopt the profession of photography and prepare myself to take over the family business."

Eva, who knew little or nothing about the subject, listened to the photographer and Hitler discuss art and was impressed by their knowledge. She was only seventeen but that night she learned a lesson. She discovered that if she were to attract the interest of Hitler she would have to cater to his likes and dislikes. In order to break into the conversation, she told Hitler about her examination of the file of photographs in the studio dealing with his career in politics. She emphasized the way the women of Germany were attracted to him. Hitler was delighted by her remarks.

"My bride is Germany," he told her. This was a statement that he was to make many times during his life. Eva was not exactly certain what he meant, but Hoffmann, who understood that Hitler was saying he would never marry because his country took the place of a wife in his heart, protested.

"Herr Hitler, you have but to make your choice. No woman would turn you down."

Hitler smiled, took Eva by the arm and walked away.

What Hoffmann and many others who knew Hitler didn't realize was that Hitler had already met a woman who had a special place in his heart—Geli Raubal, his niece, who was living at his Prinzregentenstrasse apartment.

Eva knew nothing about Geli Raubal. In fact, if anyone had told her that night that Hitler had a young mistress she wouldn't have believed it. To her, he was not the type who would have a mistress. She noticed that when Hoffmann told one of his customary vulgar stories, Hitler blushed and guided her out of the room before the story was completed. Eva was amused. She had heard most of the stories many times before at the studio, and they didn't embarrass her in the least, but it was obvious they embarrassed Hitler. Later she was to learn that though Hitler enjoyed obscene stories and pornography of all types, he didn't believe women should listen to such stories in public. In private, it was another matter.

After their first meeting in Hoffmann's home, Hitler often requested the photographer to arrange other meetings with Eva. Hoffmann told Hitler's personal adjutant, Julius Schaub, that he thought Hitler was interested in the young girl.

"Often when he intends to stop at our house for an hour or so he suggests that I ask Eva to come over because she amuses him," the photographer said. "At other times when we are at the Café Heck he will ask me to give her a ring at the studio and tell her he is going to stop by and talk with her."

Schaub just smiled. The adjutant was one of the few persons who was aware of Geli's presence in Hitler's apartment and the affair going on between uncle and niece.

Despite his affair with Geli, however, Hitler continued to see Eva and to send her flowers, candy and trinkets of modest value. Hoffmann had mixed emotions about the growing friendship between his employee and his idol. If the relationship developed into a permanent association, he knew that Hitler would remember who had introduced him to Eva and be grateful. On the other hand, he had hoped that Hitler would fall in love with his daughter Henriette. "Henny," as she was known to her friends, had inherited many of her father's less desirable traits and by the time she was seventeen had had a great deal more experience with men than Eva. Much of her time was spent with the male students at the University of Munich, teaching them some "gymnastics" they had never known but were delighted to learn. At one time Hitler had been attracted to Henny, and she had reciprocated to the fullest extent at the urging of her father. But after a short time Hitler lost interest. When the despondent Hoffmann tried to discover what went wrong, Henny wasn't much help. She swore that she had tried to please Hitler in every way possible but that after a platonic kiss or two he had turned away from her. In desperation Hoffmann then asked another close acquaintance of Adolf Hitler, Ernst

Hanfstängl (who later fled Germany and Hitler), about Hitler's sexual prowess.

Hanfstängl, who had watched Hitler's brief attempt to become friendly with his own sister Erna, had definite ideas about Hitler's sexual practices, but in 1929—while he was still a member of the intimate circle—he had no intention of making these ideas public. He merely shrugged his shoulder and muttered, "Perhaps he concentrates too much on politics to be interested in women."

Hoffmann finally decided that Henny was not going to become Hitler's favorite and concentrated on promoting Eva, hoping that if Eva found favor with him he would get his deserved reward.

"Civilian" Adolf Hitler, probably taken before he became Chancellor of Germany.

3. A Dangerous Love

Eva understood Hitler's moods and knew he could be extremely irrational in dealing with others. Hitler was a violent man.

Eva Braun eventually learned about Geli Raubal and Hitler. As her interest in Hitler increased and she spent more time with him, she learned a great deal about the niece-in-residence. No one knows for certain just when Eva decided to do everything possible to establish herself as Hitler's favorite. For several years many thought that she became his mistress only because of the circumstances, but a detailed study of the love affair reveals this is far from the truth. Eva pursued her plan to conquer Hitler so cleverly that no one, not even the jealous and

Adolf Hitler, a photo said to have been one of Eva's favorites.

greedy associates who surrounded Hitler during the Third Reich era, realized what she had in mind. In 1930 Eva recognized Geli Raubal as the most formidable obstacle in her way and decided that somehow she had to be eliminated as a rival for Hitler's attention.

Geli also knew about Eva, although it is not known when she found out. Ada Dort, who became acquainted with Geli when they both took voice lessons from Adolf Vogel, thought it was in February, 1931.

"We were walking in the English Gardens after finishing our voice lessons with Herr Vogel," she said, "and I asked Geli how she was getting along with Hitler. She took several photographs from her handbag and gave them to me. All but one were of Hitler. The last was a photograph of a very pretty girl. When I asked Geli who the girl was she blushed, grabbed the picture from my hand and put it in her pocket. It was obvious that she had given that picture to me by mistake. I remember that it was inscribed along the border in neat handwriting: 'To Adi with love, Eva.' "

Later, when the two girls parted, Geli took Ada Dort's hand in hers and apologized for her rudeness. "That girl is a friend of my uncle's. I don't like her."

Hitler's apartment in Munich was divided into two wings: Hitler lived in one and Geli supposedly lived in the other. Actually, she stayed near Hitler's bedroom in a room luxuriously furnished with antiques from Austria, several paintings (including one Hitler had done during World War I), an expensive radio-phonograph with a large supply of records, bedroom furniture with painted motifs and embroidered sheets. Hitler's bedroom, down a long corridor from Geli's, was smaller, although it too was well appointed. Geli's mother slept in a room across from the anteroom to her daughter's chamber and the two shared a bathroom. Frau Annie Winter and her husband managed the servants while Geli's mother (Hitler's half-sister Angela) was in overall charge of the household.

In 1930 Geli was twenty-two years old, four years older than Eva Braun. Hitler had first become acquainted with her when she and his half-sister joined him at Haus Wachenfeld, his mountain retreat south of Munich. After acquiring the Prinzregentenstrasse apartment, he made certain that she and her mother moved to Munich with him. He would much rather have left his half-sister back in the mountain retreat, but Hitler was conscious of his public image and wanted the citizens of Bavaria and Germany to believe that he had no time to waste on private affairs.

This subterfuge only duped his acquaintances temporarily, however. By the beginning of 1931 it was common knowledge in Munich that Hitler and Geli were having an affair that had the unpleasant suggestion of incest. They often appeared together at social functions, and Hitler made no attempt to hide his feeling for her.

There is ample evidence that, contrary to general belief, Geli was as agreeable to the affair as Hitler. She was a sexually aggressive young girl who flirted with every man she met and went to bed with many of them when she was certain her uncle would not know about it. The "prisoner-in-the-room" theory that has existed through the years has no basis in fact. Frau Winter, the housekeeper, has verified that Geli had her own key to the room and that she was free to come and go as she pleased. Geli traveled back and forth alone between her voice instructor's studio and the apartment quite often, and if she decided to take a train to Vienna, as many say she sometimes wanted to do, there was really nothing to stop her. Hitler always provided her with ample money for the best clothes, jewelry and other things she wanted, so it would

Eva never lost her love for exercise and for keeping in shape.

have been easy for her to buy a train ticket if she were trying to escape from him. The truth is that she didn't want to leave Hitler, for she was delighted with the celebrity status of her uncle—which permitted her to bask in the limelight, too. While Hitler was not nearly so famous as he would be in later years, even in 1930 and 1931 the public was noticing him and his companions. Geli loved this attention and was willing to put up with his demands—sexual or otherwise—to keep it.

A former SA officer who guarded Hitler's apartment, Wilhelm Stocker, was very friendly with Geli. "Many times, when Hitler was away for several days at a political rally or tending to party matters in Berlin or elsewhere, Geli would see other men. Hitler would have been furious if he had known that she was out with a violin player from Augsburg or a ski instructor from Innsbruck. After she was satisfied that I wouldn't tell her uncle—and I had a personal reason for not telling him—she often confided in me. She admitted to me that at times Hitler made her commit some acts in the privacy of her room that sickened her, but when I asked why she didn't refuse to do them, she just shrugged and said that she didn't want to lose him to some woman who would do what he wanted."

The "personal reason" that Stocker had for keeping Geli's extracurricular activities secret from Hitler was that he also enjoyed her sexual favors periodically. "She was a girl that needed attention and needed it constantly," he explained. "And she definitely wanted to remain Hitler's favorite. She was willing to do anything he asked to keep that status. At the beginning of 1931 I think she was worried that there was another woman in Hitler's life. She mentioned to me several times that her uncle didn't seem as interested in her as he once was."

The "other woman" was Eva Braun. Hitler was spending more and more time with her. Yet there was quite a difference in his treatment of the two. Hitler took Geli to plays, movies and restaurants, unconcerned about whether the public saw him with her or not. In fact, he seemed to enjoy the interest he aroused when he appeared with the blonde Geli on his arm. With Eva, however, everything was secretive. He never took her out in public and tried to keep his meetings with her concealed from even his closest friends. If he took Eva to Hoffmann's for the evening, he made certain that no one else except the photographer and his family was there. When he took her home he would have Erich Kempka, his chauffeur, drop her off at her parents' apartment. There, Hitler would bid her good night and leave, in case anyone was watching. Within the next hour he would meet her again at a prearranged rendezvous and spend the rest of the evening with her alone.

As Hitler's popularity and prestige increased during 1931, Geli and Eva fought harder to win his favor. Even though the two girls never met formally, they had the opportunity to observe each other at various times. One occasion occurred when Hoffmann took Eva to *Fasching* (the Munich Carnival) in March, 1931. As they entered one of the festive beer tents, Hoffmann saw

Hitler and Geli sitting at a table. He guided Eva to a table at the opposite side of the tent, not wanting the two girls to confront each other. Tactless and crude as usual, Hoffmann introduced Eva to people in the tent as "my niece," an obvious allusion to the relationship between Hitler and Geli. When this remark was passed on to Geli she was furious.

"I don't want to be put in the same class as that monkey-faced girl," she muttered. She knew that Hoffmann's companion was Eva Braun. She had seen Eva's photograph in the window at Hoffmann's studio.

Although Hitler managed to keep his budding romance with Eva concealed from nearly everyone else, Geli became more and more aware of it during the spring and summer of 1931. When his trips to Hoffmann's became more frequent, Geli was forced to spend most of her time in her room waiting for him. Occasionally she tried to go out to other parties when Hitler was away for the evening, but Hitler became furious over this. Frau Winter often heard Geli and Hitler arguing that summer, but she thought little of it since they always "kissed and made up" the following day. The arguments were occasioned by the mutual jealousy of Hitler and Geli. In August, 1931, however, Frau Winter heard Geli screaming at Hitler about a letter she had found in his coat pocket. At that time she didn't pay much attention to the incident. Later she realized that the letter was

an important factor in the tragedy that soon occurred.

Less than a month after the argument over the letter, Hitler began a campaign tour to the north of Germany. He invited Hoffmann to go along, since he wanted maximum press and photo coverage. When Hoffmann arrived at the Prinzregentenstrasse apartment on September 17, 1931, Hitler was still packing, Geli was helping him and, as usual, the two were arguing. The photographer was accustomed to these fights, so he ignored the yelling and screaming as he drank a glass of wine. Suddenly he heard Hitler tell the girl to "shut up" in a loud voice, and a moment later he came down the steps and motioned to Hoffmann that he was ready to leave. They joined the driver of the black Mercedes-Benz, Julius Schreck, and put their bags in the rear of the automobile. Hoffmann was just settling himself in the back seat of the Mercedes-Benz when Geli appeared on the second-floor balcony of the apartment. Hitler saw her and his face immediately turned red.

"For the last time, no!" he yelled.

Then Hitler nodded to the driver and the Mercedes-Benz started down the street. Hoffmann looked back and saw that Geli was crying.

That evening Geli went to the Munich Playhouse with Frau Schaub, wife of Hitler's personal adjutant, to see Maria Bard. According to Frau Schaub's statement later, Geli was lost in thought during most of the performance and several times she thought the girl was crying. At the intermission, however, Geli bought a drink and a choco-

Eva was skilled on the bars, and she exercised constantly on the Obersalzberg, at her villa, and at the various resorts she visited.

late bar at the refreshment stand and seemed more cheerful. During the ride home she spoke only when Frau Schaub spoke to her. Before she went into the apartment Geli asked what Frau Schaub intended to do during the next few days, since she knew her husband was going to join Hitler. Frau Schaub explained that she

had no definite plans. "I will be in my apartment if you get lonely."

Frau Schaub realized that Geli was upset but wasn't particularly concerned, thinking that the girl was merely bored. The next morning at 10 A.M., however, Frau Winter called to inquire whether Geli had stayed overnight with her, and if so, whether she was still at the Schaub apartment. When Frau Schaub said no, Frau Winter explained that when she had taken Geli the morning newspaper, as was her custom, there was no answer to her knock on the bedroom door. Frau Winter next called Geli's mother, who was on vacation on the Obersalzberg, and discovered that Geli was not there either. She then notified her husband, and together they forced the door to Geli's bedroom open. Geli was lying on the floor. She was dead, shot through the heart. Hitler's Walther 6.35 pistol was in her hand.

Frau Winter, loyal to Hitler while he was alive and to his memory after his death, understood immediately what she had to do. She notified Rudolf Hess, at that time the second most powerful man in the Nazi organization, and then called the police and a doctor. Hess arrived at the scene within minutes, talked briefly with Frau Winter and then placed an emergency telephone call to the Deutscher Hof Hotel in Nuremberg. As soon as Hitler arrived at the hotel the message was given to him and he immediately returned to Munich.

While no formal steps were taken to investigate Geli's death, the Munich newspapers—as yet unafraid of Adolf Hitler—gave the suicide extensive publicity. A motive was never officially established, but Maja Kempka, the attractive wife of Hitler's chauffeur, stated after Hitler's death that she once saw a pile of letters Hitler's secretary was filing, and among the letters were several from Eva Braun to Hitler. Frau Kempka believed Geli found these letters, became depressed, thinking she was losing Hitler, and killed herself.

Within three weeks after Geli's death, Adolf Hitler was seeing Eva Braun frequently. Eva now had her man to herself.

Even on her trips, Eva took every opportunity she could to swim; here she is at Garda in Italy.

4. Mistress of A Chancellor

Hitler became Chancellor of the Third Reich on January 30, 1933, through a clever plan of backstairs political intrigue. His ruthlessness soon became apparent.

Eva had worked late the night before and was still sleeping at 1 P.M. on January 30, 1933, when Fanny Braun knocked on her bedroom door and called, "Eva, wake up. I have news for you. Herr Hitler has come to power!"

When Eva learned that Hitler had been named Chancellor that morning in Berlin she was shocked. The last time Hitler had talked with her he admitted that the future of his Nazi Party looked bleak. He was depressed by the elections of November, 1932, when his party had lost more than two million votes and thirty-four seats in the Reichstag. Both the Nationalists and the Communists had gained seats, making the

defeat of the Nazis even more bitter. Eva asked herself the question thousands of other Germans were asking that January afternoon: "What happened?"

The answer was complicated.

Despite his frustration after the elections, Hitler realized that he still controlled the largest party in Germany and that the present Chancellor, Franz von Papen, would have to compromise with the Nazis on some issues whether he wanted to or not. Papen did make some conciliatory offers to Hitler in an effort to get the support of the

An official picture of Adolf Hitler, the Führer of Germany, taken in 1935.

Nazis and maintain a ruling majority in the Reichstag, but Hitler refused them and sat tight. It was a smart move. Unable to get majority support, Papen resigned, and General Kurt von Schleicher became the new Chancellor with President Paul von Hindenburg's blessing.

During this trying period Eva kept encouraging Hitler, despite her lack of expertise in politics. Paul Harns, a former waiter at the Carlton Hotel in Munich, often heard her telling Hitler that "it is always darkest before the dawn" and trying to shake him out of his depression.

"I remember a few days before Christmas, 1932, Eva and I both tried to get Hitler to celebrate the holiday with us," Harns said. "He refused, and when he said that he was going back to Berlin to see Schleicher instead, we both knew that he had decided to rejoin the political battle. We looked at each other, thinking that perhaps we had convinced him. That Eva could have convinced a man of anything. She was some woman!"

Another witness to Eva's confidence in Hitler's great political future during December, 1932 was Maria Paith, a hostess and waitress at the Osteria Bavaria in Munich, a small café Hitler frequented. She knew Eva well, since their families lived only one block apart, but was unaware that Eva was Hitler's mistress. She thought that Eva accompanied Hitler to the café because she was employed by Hoffmann and Hoffmann was a close friend of Hitler's. Once, after she had heard Eva telling Hitler that "if he quit the political battle he was a coward," she warned her not to speak that way to him.

"If you make him angry," she said," he will take his business away from Hoffmann and you may lose your job. Hitler is a monster when he gets angry."

Eva just smiled and told Maria not to worry.

Just how much influence Eva exerted on Hitler at this low period in his political career cannot be estimated, but by early December he was back in the thick of the political fracas in Berlin. When the new Chancellor Schleicher failed to win a majority in the Reichstag, Hitler's position improved—despite the fact that President Hindenburg considered him a radical unfit for a high position in the government of Germany. With neither Papen nor Schleicher able to form a ruling caucus and all government business at a standstill, even Hindenburg knew that action must be taken. The climax came on the night of January 29, 1933, the night Eva worked late at the Hoffmann studio in Munich. As she sorted photographs of Hitler and other Nazi leaders, a different sorting process was going on in and around Berlin.

Schleicher, in a last-stand maneuver, sent a representative to Hitler at the home of Hélène Bechstein in Charlottenburg, to warn Hitler that Papen intended to ask for the Chancellorship again. Schleicher suggested that he and Hitler form a coalition to rule with the combined support of the German Army and the Nazis. Hitler ig-

Eva and Adolf holding a private conversation at the Berghof.

nored the suggestion. A few hours later Hitler learned that Schleicher was preparing a putsch with the support of the German Army and intended to kidnap the President and declare military law! Hitler alerted his private army, the SA, and warned Papen and Hindenburg of the plot. It was a long night for everyone concerned. Hindenburg, old and weary, finally decided that the only alternative to chaos was to give the "radical" Hitler a chance to form a government and name him Chancellor— but on the condition that General von Blomberg, the President's trusted friend, become Minister of Defense. The next morning Blomberg arrived in Berlin from Geneva, where he had been serving as chief military adviser to the German delegation at the Disarmament Conference. He accepted the offer, and Hitler received the long-awaited summons from Hindenburg. Shortly after noon on January 30, 1933, Adolf Hitler was named Chancellor of Germany.

Eva congratulated herself on her position as the favorite female companion of the new Chancellor, but there was no one to whom she could brag. Though her mother now admitted that perhaps she had underestimated Hitler, she still did not suspect how well her daughter actually knew him. She only knew that Eva was the caretaker of the Hitler photographic file at Hoffmann's studio and that she often had to meet Hitler at the studio and other places "on busi-

Eva (kneeling, right) and Hitler, shown at the wedding party of her friend Marion Schoenemann.

ness.'' But she was quick to tell the neighbors that ''Eva knows the Chancellor'' and to garner any prestige this might bring the Braun family. At first Eva was amused, then worried. Hitler was now Germany's man of the hour and all eyes were on him. His every move was followed religiously by newspaper reporters, supporters, enemies and plain citizens, and Eva knew that her presence at his side would be noted and duly reported. She was worried about how she would explain to her parents that she was more than just a keeper of Hitler's photograph file, that she was actually the new Chancellor's mistress.

Eva needn't have worried about publicity concerning their affair, for Hitler had no intention of allowing the citizens of Germany to find out about her. As he told Hoffmann, ''The *chère amie* of a politician must be quietly discreet.'' But though Hitler wanted to impress upon the German people that he was too dedicated to governing the country and leading it back to prewar eminence to have time for a serious love affair, he secretly planned to continue his relationship with Eva. Certainly he thought of Eva immediately after his ascension to power, for he placed a telephone call to her that night. The scene in Berlin was hectic. As the news spread throughout the city, a vast crowd of Hitler's supporters and curious onlookers surrounded the Kaiserhof Hotel where he was meeting with his party officials. Later he went to the Chancellery and saluted the thousands of SA, SS and armed forces personnel who paraded past the building for hours carrying torches. Thousands of telephone calls from all over the world jammed the Chancellery switchboards. Nearly one hundred requests for a telephone line to the Chancellery came from the United States alone that January night. Even for the new Chancellor it wasn't easy to obtain a telephone line, but in the midst of the wild celebrations, the conferences with Göring, Goebbels, Blomberg and others and the multitude of calls and telegrams, Hitler spoke to Eva in Munich.

It soon became obvious to Eva that Hitler did not intend to allow their affair to become public knowledge, but this secrecy did not solve her personal problems. As soon as he returned to Munich after becoming Chancellor, Hitler invited Eva to his apartment and, with the assurance born of success, insisted that she stay all night. As Frau Winter said frankly, ''He received many women but none of them ever stayed all night except Eva Braun.''

Such visits became more and more frequent, as did the luncheon and dinner dates at the Osteria Bavaria and the Carlton Hotel. At these public places Hitler was always accompanied by party officials so that the public never noticed Eva in particular. If her presence was questioned, it was quickly explained that she was a representative of the Hoffmann studio, conferring with Hitler about pictures to be distributed. Though such explanations satisfied the public, at home Eva was having more and more problems in her attempts to conceal her true relationship with Hitler. Her strict and uncompromising father could not understand her irregular hours, nor why she "stayed overnight at a friend's house" so often—especially since she never explained who the "friend" was or where she lived. Neither did he understand why Eva insisted on having her own telephone in her bedroom and allowed no one to answer it but herself. Ilse knew why Eva wanted the telephone and often heard her sister having long conversations with Hitler while hiding under the blankets to muffle her voice. Ilse didn't want to get involved, however, because she was working for a Jewish doctor and suspected Hitler wouldn't appreciate that fact. Ilse didn't like Hitler, but at the same time she didn't blame her sister for being friendly with the Chancellor of Germany.

Eva's youngest sister Gretl knew she was having "quite an affair" with some man because of the secret telephone calls and her overnight visits at a "friend's house." She didn't know who the man was, but, being of a romantic age, she was in favor of her sister's adventure. Thus Eva was able to keep her affair secret from her parents temporarily, even though all three Braun daughters shared one bedroom.

Gradually the web of deception became quite complicated, especially after Hitler began inviting Eva to Haus Wachenfeld on the Obersalzberg. On these occasions Eva had to be away from home for the entire weekend, since the trip from Munich took several hours. At first she told her parents that Hoffmann insisted she attend to some business for him over the weekend, and her father would reluctantly give her permission to go—although he denounced Hoffmann as a very thoughtless boss. Eva would pack her small suitcase and walk to the intersection of Turkenstrasse, where one of Hitler's black Mercedes-Benz limousines would be waiting for her. When she returned on Sunday night from Haus Wachenfeld, the secret procedure was reversed. Hitler himself never came near the Braun apartment. Despite his acclaim as the new savior of Germany, he seemed to fear a confrontration with Fritz Braun as much as Eva did. Though the situation was agonizing for Eva, she was determined not to relinquish Hitler regardless of the consequences.

In other ways the period immediately after Hitler's appointment as Chancellor was enjoyable for Eva. Now that he no longer had to spend so much time trying to become Chancellor and devising stratagems to beat out such men as Papen or Schleicher, he had more time for her. He had the power to issue orders, and party members would take care of the details. Now the police of the country protected his privacy instead of invading it. He had a fleet of planes, several automobiles, special trains—any type of transportation he wanted—and Eva accompanied him on many trips. When Eva celebrated her twenty-first birthday less than a week after his ascension to power, he bought her a complete set of tourmaline jewelry. Though it was not really expensive jewelry, it was the best she had ever owned. Before her death Eva had a wide choice of precious jewelry, but the tourmalines remained her

These photos reveal the growing intimacy between Eva and Adolf, with all pretense of "friendship" dissipated. On the left, they leave the Berghof together.

sentimental favorites the rest of her life.

As proud as she was of the birthday gift, she couldn't allow her parents to see it. This and the other nagging irritations surrounding her secret affair bothered Eva. She loved her parents. The obligation to obey them made her feel guilty every time she deceived them. She finally decided that she had to bring Fritz and Fanny Braun face to face with Adolf Hitler. When she heard her father state at dinner one evening that while he didn't care for Hitler's ideas or his political radicalism, "the man must have something or Hindenburg would not have shaken hands with him," Eva had her first glimmer of encouragement.

Every time Hitler made a speech Eva turned on the radio in the Braun apartment, and despite his opposition Fritz Braun listened. At first he criticized nearly everything Hitler proposed or did, but as unemployment was eased across the country and living conditions improved he began to weaken. Once or twice within Eva's hearing he even made complimentary remarks about Hitler. Eva then decided the time had come to introduce her parents to Hitler and tell them the truth.

The Brauns often took automobile excursions on Sundays, and one day Eva heard her father suggest they drive south to Berchtesgaden and go up into the mountains, since they had not been in the area for quite a while. Fanny Braun agreed, and early the next Sunday morning the Brauns and their friends headed toward the Obersalzberg. They had asked Eva and Gretl to go along but both refused, which didn't surprise the parents since neither girl traveled with them much anymore.

Eva had already planned to drive to Haus Wachenfeld with Hitler's entourage and this gave her the opportunity she had been waiting for. She knew her parents often stopped at the Lambacher Hof, in the small town of Lambach between Munich and Berchtesgaden, for tea and a snack. If she could get Hitler to stop there also, perhaps she could finally introduce him to her parents. Coincidentally, that Sunday while the Brauns were on the Obersalzberg, Fanny Braun suggested they go see Hitler's house in the mountains. "The people talk so much about the house," she said, "I would like to see it."

The Brauns were both surprised at the size of the house—it was quite small. (They would see it many times in later years when it was much more elaborate and called "Berghof.") A large crowd had gathered in front of it that Sunday, all shouting, "We want to see our Führer! We want to see our Führer!" Frau Braun turned to her husband and said, "Let's go. *I* don't want to see him."

As Eva had predicted, the Brauns and their friends decided to stop in Lambach on the return trip to Munich. When they reached the town, however, they discovered that the road was guarded by SS troops who wanted to know where they were going. The troops explained that "the Führer is on his way through Lambach" and strict security measures had been ordered. After Herr Braun explained that they were merely going to the Lambacher Hof for a snack, the SS officer in charge of the roadblock motioned them to pass. The number of SS troops and the excitement of the townspeople were the main topic of conversation among the Brauns and their companions as they sat in the café. They had just finished their tea and were about to leave when a shiny Mercedes-Benz drove up to the main entrance, and their daughter Eva stepped from the back seat. Fanny Braun could not believe her eyes, but a second long look convinced her that the girl was really Eva. She hurried to her daughter's side and exclaimed, "Eva, you?"

Eva smiled at her mother but said nothing.

By this time Fritz Braun had recovered from his shock and had joined his wife near the Mercedes-Benz. "Where have you come from? What does this mean?"

Very quietly Eva said, "I have come from Haus Wachenfeld." Without another word she brushed past her mother and father and disappeared into the Lambacher Hof. At that moment another Mercedes-Benz stopped at the café and Hitler stepped out. As the townspeople cheered and crowded around his car in order to see him better, Fanny Braun edged away from the scene. Now that she knew Eva was more than just a casual friend of the Führer's she wanted time to think, to decide what she and her husband should do. Fritz Braun, however, did not move. When Hitler walked past him he extended his hand. "I am Eva's father."

He expected an explanation from Hitler but he received none.

"And where is your Frau Gemahlin?" Hitler asked.

Fritz Braun looked around in the crowd but he could not find his wife. Meanwhile Hitler and his entourage moved on into the Lambacher Hof. When Herr Braun finally located his wife she said, "Let's go immediately." She now understood why Eva had talked so much about "our Führer" and why she had always urged her parents to have faith in him. She wanted to get home quickly so she could analyze the situation by herself. Just as she and her husband reached their automobile, however, Hitler's adjutant came onto the porch of the Lambacher Hof.

"Where are the Braun parents, please?"

Fanny Braun turned her back on the inquiring adjutant and murmured to her husband, "I don't want to go in."

Fritz Braun convinced her that it would be best if they did. They were ushered into the private dining room where Hitler and Eva were eating. Hitler immediately stood up and motioned for Frau Braun to take the vacant chair next to his. After he shook her hand, Fanny Braun sat down and Hitler began talking. He never mentioned Eva. He spoke about the beauty of the mountains, the cakes, the tea, and other trivial subjects. Later Frau Braun came to realize the special effort Hitler had put out that day, since he rarely "chatted." In fact—as she deduced that Sunday afternoon—he was a very poor conversationalist unless he was giving a monologue on his political, racial or military ideas. Frau Braun was very attentive and waited for Hitler to speak some serious words about Eva, whom he called *du* sev-

Alone together, they are obviously enjoying each other's company, looking down at Berchtesgaden.

Eva, self-appointed "queen" of the Berghof, discussing matters of construction; she considered it her personal dominion.

The door led to Hitler's bedroom; Eva's apartment had a door into his sleeping quarters.

eral times at the table, but the words never came. When it was time to leave, Hitler took Fanny Braun's hand and kept her in the dining room a few moments after the others had departed. He squeezed her hand hard three times and, as Fanny Braun told her husband later, "He looked straight through me as though he could look into my very soul." Hitler never spoke a word while he held her hand but she had the impression that he was trying to comfort her.

The meeting between her parents and Hitler had come off just as she had desired, but Eva didn't know what to expect from them when she arrived home. She was happy they knew the truth, that she would no longer have to deceive them. However, if it came to a showdown between her parents and Hitler, Hitler was her choice. She was deeply infatuated with him and had no intention of giving him up. She had fought too hard and too long to reach her present position in his life to allow parental objections to interfere. It was her life and she intended to live it as she pleased.

When she returned to the Braun apartment that night her father was waiting for her. "Is it true that you are the Führer's mistress?"

Eva didn't answer him directly. "If you want, I'll leave."

Fritz Braun turned and walked away.

Eva and Adolf out for a walk in the mountains around the Berghof.

5. Eva's Diary

"It is hell to be twenty-two years old and in love with a man twice your age, and still not know whether he is in love with you or not."

Eva Braun faced the year of 1935 with a great deal of uncertainty and disillusionment. During the past two years, her romance with Hitler had progressed satisfactorily to a certain point but was now stalemated. She felt no doubt that Hitler was more attached to her now than when they had first met, but she could not become accustomed to his long periods of neglect. She had thought that once they became this close he would keep her at his side constantly and grow more attentive to her needs and her feelings—but he did not.

Hitler's lack of ardor was emotionally painful to Eva; it was also embarrassing. Ilse knew whenever Hitler failed to visit or send for Eva for weeks at a time, and she often remarked how rude and thoughtless he was. Her mother and father usually wore knowing looks on their faces during these periods of neglect. But humiliation in front of her family was something Eva could endure. What she could not stand was the thought of losing Hitler. Every time she read in the newspaper that the Chancellor had attended the opera in Berlin or a musical concert at Bayreuth, she wondered who had been with him. Often a picture

In the early days of Eva's friendship with Hitler, she spent long, lonely hours waiting for his attention, trying to find a way to occupy herself and forget her misery.

provided the answer—a beautiful actress—which only worried her more. She never ceased to hate her "backstreet" existence, and in 1935, when she was not as sure of her position with Hitler as she was to be in later years, his public association with other women made her extremely jealous and angry.

To be angry and have no one to argue with was frustrating. Eva's increasing isolation from friends and family left her too much time to imagine what was happening in Berlin while she waited in Munich. Gradually she became more and more depressed about Hitler's indifference and expressed her growing disillusionment in her diary:

February 6, 1935. *I guess today is the right day to begin this masterpiece. I have happily reached my twenty-third year, that is. Whether I am happy is another question. At the moment I certainly am not happy. That is because I have such expectations of such an important day. If I only had a dog, then I wouldn't be quite so alone, but I guess that is asking too much.*

Frau Schaub [wife of Hitler's adjutant Julius Schaub] *came with flowers and a telegram as an "ambassador." My whole office looks like a flower shop and smells like a mortuary. I really am ungrateful, but I had hoped so much to get a little Dachshund and now—again nothing. Perhaps next year or even after that. Then it will be better suited to an incipient spinster.*

Let me not give up hope. I should have learned patience by now.

I bought two lottery tickets today because I was convinced it was now or never. They were blanks. It seems as though I'll never get rich. Can't do anything about it.

Today I was to go to the Zugspitze with Herta, Gretl, Ilse and mother, and we would have lived like queens because one always has the most fun when others share the happiness. But the trip didn't come off.

Today I'm going to eat with Herta. What else may a simple little woman of twenty-three do? Thus I'll bring my birthday to a close with gluttony. I believe I shall then have acted in accordance with his preferences.

Obviously Eva was feeling sorry for herself. She had hinted to Hitler many times that she wanted a dog to keep her company during the long hours she had to sit and wait for him, but on her twenty-third birthday she received nothing, "again." The bouquet and telegram brought by his "ambassador" Frau Schaub were small comfort to a romantic young girl who desperately wanted to be with her lover. Frau Schaub had had experience in trying to comfort Hitler's girlfriends before. It was she who had taken Geli Raubal to the Munich Playhouse on the night before Geli committed suicide. She liked Eva, so she stayed and talked to her about how busy the Chancellor was with his multitude of problems. Instead of feeling depressed, she pointed out, Eva should be proud that such

Though Eva often traveled with Hitler, she was frequently barred from being seen with him. Here, in Italy, she stops to feed a donkey.

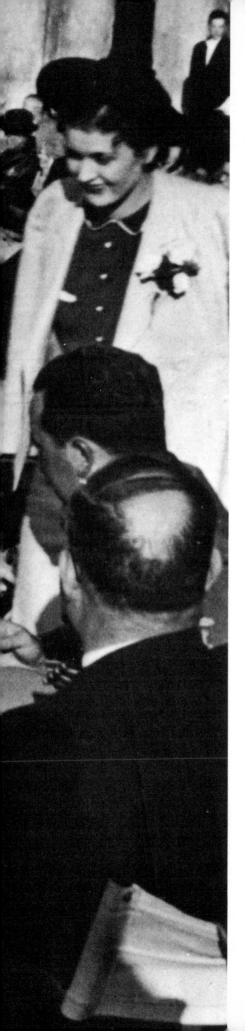

Eva, enjoying the sunshine, has tea with friends on a trip to Italy. She is also shown, silhouetted against the setting sun, during a cruise off Naples. Sightseeing, alone in a crowd—also at Naples—while Hitler presumably took care of business.

a busy man, such a great man, had taken time to send her flowers and a telegram.

Hitler was indeed busy in February, 1935. The British and French governments had renewed their efforts to persuade Germany to agree on mutual assistance in case of war with Russia or another country in Eastern Europe. Hitler was opposed to such an agreement; he was not afraid of any nation attacking Germany at that time, so why, he asked the Reichstag, should he pledge to help others if they were attacked? However, Germany's forbidden rearmament had reached such proportions that it could no longer be concealed. Hitler knew that if he agreed to the mutual assistance pact the Western powers would overlook Germany's secret rearming. He was still trying to work out a solution on Eva's birthday, and it was impossible for him to fly to Munich to see her.

Five days later Hitler did go to Munich.

> February 11, 1935. *He was just here, but no dog and no clothes. He didn't even ask me whether I had a birthday wish. So now I have bought myself some jewelry. A necklace, earrings, and a ring to match for fifty marks. Everything very pretty. I hope he likes it. If not he can buy me something himself.*

After this visit Eva was temporarily placated and happier than she had been for some time. According to the next entry in her diary, she was confident that she and an acquaintance named Charlotte ("Charlie") would be invited to Berlin to stay with Hitler for a while:

> February 15, 1935. *It seems that the Berlin deal is really going to come off. I won't believe it until I am in the Reich Chancellery. I hope it'll be an agreeable affair. Too bad Herta can't come along instead of Charlie. She would guarantee a few happy days. This way there will probably be a big ado, because I don't think Brückner will show his more charming side for Charlie. I don't dare look forward to it yet, but it might turn out to be wonderful if everything goes well. Let's hope so.*

Three days later Hitler stopped in Munich again and paid a visit to Eva. It is apparent from this date's entry in her diary that it was often difficult for him to contact her at the Braun apartment. Chancellor or not, he still had not been accepted by Fritz and Fanny Braun, so he never visited Eva at home. In 1935 the man whom much of the world was warily watching, who was feared by large numbers of Germans, shied away from a confrontration with Eva's parents. To Hitler's coarse, rigid mind it was best to avoid the parents of his mistress, because they made him feel uncomfortable. This was a quirk in his personality, a throwback to the Germanic parental disciplinary attitude of past years when the father of the girl decided whether the man she wanted to associate with was suitable. The fear he had had of his own father in his youth made him hesitant to face Eva's father in 1935. So Eva's suggestion that she should have a place of her own where she could meet him whenever he desired impressed Hitler favorably.

February 18, 1935. *Yesterday he came quite unexpectedly, and it was a delightful evening. The nicest thing was that he is thinking about taking me out of the studio and—I don't want to be too happy yet— buy me a little house. I don't dare think of it. It would be so wonderful. I wouldn't have to open the door for our "honorable" customers and play salesgirl. Dear God, please make it come true within a reasonable period of time.*

Poor Charlie is sick and can't come to Berlin with us. She's really sick but maybe it is better that way. Maybe he would be very rude to her and then she would certainly be even more unhappy.

I am so infinitely happy. Happy that he loves me so and pray that it will always be like this. I should never want to be blamed if he should stop loving me.

Eva felt it was absurd that she had to play the part of a salesgirl to cover up their romance. It was ironic that Hitler, who now had millions of marks at his disposal, controlled the German Army, was in complete charge of his country's political and domestic affairs and was making his presence felt in international politics, continued to slip in and out of Hoffmann's studio to see her and to arrange highly clandestine meetings at Hoffmann's home or at his own Prinzregentenstrasse apartment. This situation depressed Eva for two important reasons. It made her status with Hitler ambiguous. As she often told Paul Harns, if Hitler really cared for her he would provide her with her own apartment and drop these elaborate subterfuges. Also, she feared he was only

using her and would eventually replace her with another woman. The fact that he didn't want the public or even his party members to know about their relationship emphasized its precariousness. As her diary entry of February 18, 1935 indicates, she was overjoyed that Hitler had finally mentioned the possibility of arranging for her to have her own "little house." Her fervent statement that "I should never want to be blamed if he should stop loving me" expresses her firm intention to do everything he desired.

Though she was happy when she wrote those lines in her diary, the feeling didn't last long.

March 4, 1935. *I am again mortally unhappy. Since I can't write him, this book must serve to assuage my pain. He came Saturday when the town of Munich's ball took place. Frau Schwarz [wife of the party treasurer] had given me a loge ticket for it and so I was obliged to attend at all costs since I had already accepted. Thus I spent a few wonderful hours with him until 12:00 midnight and then went to the ball for two hours with his permission.*

He promised that I would see him on Sunday. In spite of the fact that I called up from the Osteria and that I sent a message that I am waiting for his news, he simply drove off to Feldafing. He even refused Hoffmann's invitation to tea and supper. One may look at everything from two sides: perhaps he wanted to be alone with Dr. Goebbels who was also here, but he could have informed me. I was at Hoffmann's on pins and needles thinking that he might come into the studio at any minute.

We went to the train station because we learned that he had suddenly decided to leave but only arrived in time to see the rear lights of the departing train. Hoffmann had once again left home with us too late so I couldn't even say goodbye. Probably I'm too pessimistic again, I hope, but he hasn't been here now for fourteen days and I am so unhappy that I have no peace of mind. I don't know why he should be mean to me. Perhaps on account of the ball, but he gave me permission to go. I am uselessly wracking my brain as to why he should be going away without saying goodbye.

Hoffmann gave me a ticket for tonight's performance of Venetian Nights *but I'm not going. I am much too unhappy.*

Whenever Hitler did not get his own way he became very angry. If he couldn't monopolize a conversation, he pouted. If anyone—whether a personal associate or political leader—didn't agree with him, he went into a rage. It seems he resented Eva's going to the ball even though he had given his permission. The "few wonderful hours with him" prior to the affair had not satisfied his ego. Probably he had been testing Eva by urging her to keep her appointment with Frau Schwarz, thinking that she would choose to stay with him instead. When the confused Eva went to the ball because she did not want to disappoint Frau Schwarz, Hitler decided to teach her a lesson. The diary remarks are evidence that he completely ignored Eva for a period after this incident.

March 11, 1935. I only wish one thing—to be seriously ill for at least eight days. Why doesn't something happen to me? Why do I have to suffer like this? I wish I had never seen him. I am desperate. I am going to buy more sleeping tablets. At least then I'll be half-dazed and won't think about him so much. Why doesn't the devil come and get me? I'm sure it is nicer there than here.

For three hours I stood outside the Carlton and had to watch while he brought flowers for Ondra and invited her for supper.

He is only using me for very definite purposes. When he says he loves me he takes it about as seriously as his promises, which he never keeps. Why does he torture me so much instead of just putting an end to the whole thing?

It was bad enough for Eva not to see Hitler, but when he visited Munich and didn't even call her she felt forsaken. It is evident from her diary that she desperately tried to see him—she stood outside a hotel for three hours while he dined with Anny Ondra, wife of the one-time world boxing champion, Max Schmeling. Her statement, "He is only using me for very definite purposes," must mean that when they did meet they had sexual relations, and that she now believed this constituted his only interest in her. If this were true, she realized, then her hold on him was tenu-

Hitler objected vehemently to Eva's smoking and tried to discourage her in every way he could—in vain.

ous, since he might meet another woman who was just as willing to meet his sexual demands. This knowledge only added to her depression.

> March 16, 1935. *He went to Berlin today. If only I was not beside myself when I see him less than usual. Actually it is quite natural that he shows no great interest in me at present since there is so much going on politically. I'm going to take a trip to the Zugspitze with Gretl today and I think that will put my craziness to rest. Everything has always turned out all right in the end so far and it will be the same this time. One must have patience, that's all.*

Most of her friends and associates thought that Eva knew nothing of politics, but this was not true. However, she was perceptive enough not to discuss politics with Hitler. Hitler once stated: "I detest women who dabble in politics. And if their dabbling extends to the military, it is unendurable." He often said that a man who yells and screams during a political argument in the Reichstag was "not a handsome sight," but that a woman in such a situation would be shocking. "Her voice becomes strident, she is ready to pull her hair out and her claws are showing." Hitler felt that everything that involved aggression was exclusively men's business, while women were best at training youth, decorating and caring for homes and, of course, satisfying sexual needs.

Political affairs kept Hitler busy, as Eva indicated in her diary, until April 1, 1935, when he finally visited her again. By this time his pique had faded somewhat, but he was still cool toward her.

> April 1, 1935. *Yesterday we were invited by him for supper at the Vierjahreszeite. I had to sit next to him for three hours and couldn't say a word to him. When taking leave he handed me an envelope containing money, as he had done once before. If only he had at least added a greeting or a kind word. I would have been so happy but he never thinks of anything like that.*
>
> *Why doesn't he go to Hoffmann's to eat? There at least I would have him to myself for a few minutes. I only wish he would not come any more until his home is ready.*

April was a very distressing month for Eva. Hitler's Munich apartment was being remodeled by the architect Paul Ludwig Troost, and since Hitler did not like staying in a hotel, his trips to Munich were few. He was also deeply involved in the delicate, dangerous maneuver of overseeing rearmament plans while warding off any decisive moves Great Britain or France might make in opposition. Eva, however, cared for only one fact—she was not able to see the man she loved and she missed him.

> April 29, 1935. *Things are tough. Very much so in every respect. I keep humming to myself "things will improve" but it doesn't help much. His apartment is ready but I am not allowed to go to him. Love does not seem to be on the program at present. Now that he is back in Berlin I feel a little better but there were days last week when I did my share of crying at night.*

Especially since I spent Easter at home by myself.

I'm getting on everybody's nerves because I want to sell everything from my clothes down to my photo camera and even theater tickets. After all, my debts are not that big. He's kind—and equally tactless.

During the infrequent trips Hitler made to Munich during this period he did not invite Eva to his newly remodeled apartment, nor did he arrange a meeting with her at

Eva never lost a chance to soak up sunshine, despite the fact there was still plenty of snow on the ground.

Ample evidence of Eva's passion for sunshine is revealed as she relaxes at the Königsee. Hitler often complained that Eva "showed too much flesh in public," but Eva obviously paid little attention.

Hoffmann's house. Usually he had a set procedure for his visits. On the train or plane from Berlin he would talk to associates he had invited to go with him to Munich. As soon as he arrived in Munich he would hurry to architect Troost's studio just off Theresienstrasse. Everyone would study the architect's plans, and Hitler would usually become very excited because architecture was one of his hobbies. After the studio conference he and his associates would go to the Osteria Bavaria to eat. The party at the café customarily consisted of Hitler, Hess, Bormann, Hoffmann and sometimes a painter or a sculptor. Until the Munich Ball incident Eva was also invited, but during March and April she had to stand on the street with the several hundred other persons who had heard Hitler was coming and were waiting to see him arrive at the Osteria Bavaria. She loved him so much that she endured this mortification just to get a glimpse of him, hoping he would see her in the crowd and have one of his aides ask her to join him.

It was while being jostled in the crowd around the café one day that she first saw a new feminine face among Hitler's party. It was Unity Mitford, an Englishwoman who was obsessed by Hitler and the Nazi Party.

May 2, 1935. *As Frau Hoffmann lovingly and tactlessly told me, he now has a substitute for me. Her name is Walküre [Unity Mitford's nickname] and she looks it, including her legs. But these are the shape that appeal to him. If that is true, he will soon have annoyed her until she gets slim unless she has Charlie's talent for thriving*

on worry. Worry seems to increase Charlie's appetite.

If Frau Hoffmann's observations should turn out to be true, it is mean of him not to tell me. After all he should know me well enough to realize that I would never stand in his way if he should discover another romantic interest. Why should he worry about what happens to me? I'll wait until the third of June. By then it will be three months since our last meeting. Me, supposedly the mistress of Germany's and the world's greatest man, has to look at him through a window!

He has so little understanding. He still makes me appear distant even when we are among his friends. Well, one makes his own bed. I guess it is really my fault but it is just one of those things which one likes to blame on someone else. This period of love fasting won't last forever and then it will be much better. Too bad, though, that it just happens to be spring.

By this time Eva was becoming desperate. Hitler was her first and only lover, and she felt that she was losing him. Three or four months without an intimate visit with him must mean he was losing interest. Then she saw him several times with Unity Mitford at the Osteria Bavaria and had to listen to Frau Hoffmann's malicious chatter about Hitler's "new love." Despite the "noble" remarks in her diary, Eva could not resign herself gracefully to the loss of her lover.

May 28, 1935. *I have just sent him a letter, one that is decisive for me. Will he consider it as important as I do? Well, I'll see. If I don't get an answer by ten o'clock tonight I'll take my twenty-five pills and lie down peacefully. Is it a sign of the terrific love of which he assures me that he hasn't spoken a kind word to me for three months? Agreed, he has been busy with political problems but haven't things eased off? And how about last year when he had lots of worries with Röhm and with Italy and still found time for me? True, I'm not in a position to judge whether the present situation isn't much worse but after all a few kind words at Hoffmann's would hardly have taken much time. I fear there is some other reason. It's not my fault. Certainly not. Perhaps it is another woman, although I doubt that it is the Walküre. But there are many others. What other reasons could there be?*

Lord, I'm afraid I won't get an answer today. If only someone would help me. Everything is so hopeless. Maybe my letter reached him at an inopportune time or maybe I shouldn't have written it at all. Whatever it is, the uncertainty is much worse than a sudden end would be.

Dear God, please make it possible that I speak to him today. Tomorrow will be too late. I have decided on thirty-five pills so as to make it dead certain this time. If he would at least have someone call up for him.

Immediately after mailing her ultimatum Eva began to have misgivings. At twenty-three years of age and involved in her first real love affair, she did not have much experience in handling men. There was no one she could consult—her mother or Ilse would have advised her to forget Adolf Hitler. But she did not want to forget him. She wanted to frighten him into realizing that he should love her. This tactic had worked once before, when she had wounded herself with her father's pistol during a period of depression over her relationship with Hitler. That had been three years earlier, and for a time Hitler had been much more attentive. Gradually, however, he had resumed his thoughtless ways. Now he was engaged in what he considered his greatest political mission—the reconstruction of Germany—and he probably viewed Eva's letter with some irritation as the emotional blackmail of a designing woman. In any case, she received no reply from him by the deadline to which she had committed herself.

Early on the morning of May 29, 1935, Eva laid her diary beside her bed and swallowed two dozen Phanodorm tablets. Within a few minutes she was unconscious. Fortunately, Ilse decided to return an evening gown she had borrowed from Eva and discovered her sister prostrate on the bed. She immediately called her employer, Dr. Marx. Then, drawing on her own medical experience, she gave Eva first aid. Within two hours the doctor had purged Eva of the drug and she was safe. Meanwhile, Ilse removed from Eva's diary the pages that referred to her plans to commit suicide and attempted to conceal the Jewish doctor's part in her recovery. The Nuremberg Laws had not yet been put into effect, but Ilse was aware that Hitler had already started his persecution of the Jews. She

knew he wouldn't hesitate to take action against Dr. Marx in anger or guilt over Eva's attempted suicide even though the doctor had saved her life. Ilse told their parents and Hitler that Eva was suffering from excessive fatigue and would have to stay in bed for several days. Hitler didn't question Ilse's version of the incident, but Himmler's men learned the truth within a matter of hours and the facts were relayed to the Chancellor.

Life then changed dramatically for Eva Braun. Hitler was both baffled and flattered that she had tried to kill herself over him. He realized that he had come very close to losing her, and for the first time in his life admitted to himself that he wanted her with him. He arranged for her to move into a thirty-thousand-dollar villa on the outskirts of Munich, established her as the "first lady" of the Berghof, his mountain retreat, and also provided an apartment for her in the Reich Chancellery in Berlin.

Eva was not alone any longer.

Eva with a friend having lunch at the Königsee. She was careful about her diet, always worrying about getting fat, despite the fact Hitler thought her too thin.

6. Love Under Fire

The next years were happy ones for Eva despite the start of the war in 1939. Hitler gave her a villa, she became the unchallenged mistress of the Berghof, and she had her own apartment in the Reich Chancellery near Hitler's living quarters. The Führer's interest in other women waned as his power increased. It was a happy interlude for Eva.

Now that Hitler had been proven less than invincible, many of his associates began thinking more about their own future welfare than that of the Führer and the Third Reich. Eva, however, became stronger in her support as the situation deteriorated. As others in Hitler's entourage became suspicious of one another, began to doubt the Führer's leadership and even plotted against his life, Eva tried in every way to bolster his flagging spirits and ego, to keep his appearance and posture in the image the German public expected of their Chancellor. She even tried the dangerous tactic of calming him when he flew into an uncontrollable rage. More than ever she devoted herself to him, disregarding his motives and the morality of what he was doing. When his nihilism and destructiveness backlashed on him, she was at his side.

Whenever Eva was away from Hitler he fretted constantly about her. He also began to talk about her more and more to his secretaries and other associates. One night when Eva was at her villa, an air raid on Munich was announced. Hitler "ran around like a lion in his cage and tried desperately to get in contact with Eva by telephone." Later, after he learned she was

A pensive Eva in a moment of quiet reflection, shown in the garden of her villa.

safe, he told Frau Traudl Junge, his secretary, "She doesn't go into the bunker, although I constantly ask her to do so. Her villa will some day fall in like a house of cards. Nor will she run over to my house where she would be absolutely safe. Now, I've at least brought her to the point where she has had her own bunker built at her villa, but instead of using it, she takes the whole neighborhood and goes up on the roof to see if the incendiary bombs have fallen on it. She is really a very courageous, proud woman," Hitler continued. "I have known her for more than ten years and as an employee of Hoffmann's she had to save a lot at the beginning. Yet she wouldn't permit me to pay for even a taxi. For days she slept in Hoffmann's office on a bench so that I could reach her by telephone, because she had no long-distance connection at home."

Frau Junge, since she was as young as Eva, was often included in Hitler's conversations about his mistress. After several such long talks she became more bold and asked him, "*Mein Führer*, why haven't you married?" She knew that he liked to arrange marriages between others and was interested in his associates' marriages, and she couldn't understand why he himself refused to marry.

"I wouldn't be a good head of a family," Hitler said slowly, looking at Frau Junge with his intent stare. "I would consider it irresponsible of me to start a family when I cannot devote myself to my wife sufficiently. Besides, I want no children of my own. I find that the offspring of geniuses usually have it hard in the world.

One expects of them the same importance as that of the famous predecessor and doesn't forgive them for being average. Besides, they are mostly cretins."

His devotion to Eva seemed to increase with each military defeat the German troops suffered during 1943 and 1944. While his concern for Eva grew, however, his cruelty toward others increased in direct proportion. When General Friedrich von Paulus reported in January, 1943, that 330,000 troops of his German 6th Army at Stalingrad were suffering unbearably from cold, hunger and epidemics, and that to continue fighting in such conditions was beyond human strength, Hitler refused to allow him to surrender to the Russians. Hitler's prestige as a leader meant more to him than the lives of 330,000 German soldiers. He told Paulus, "Capitulation is impossible. The 6th Army will do its historic duty at Stalingrad until the last man, in order to make possible the reconstruction of the Eastern Front." That same day he promoted Paulus to the rank of Field Marshal in an attempt to bribe him into dying on the battlefield.

But Paulus would not allow his men to suffer any longer and surrendered. When Hitler heard that Paulus had allowed himself to be taken prisoner he was furious. He felt that his prestige had suffered, and he screamed that the German generals were turning against him. "He should have killed himself, just like the old commanders who threw themselves on their swords when they saw their cause was lost."

With each defeat Hitler withdrew further from his associates. At his field headquar-

*Hitler finally gave Eva her own villa; it was on
Wasserburgerstrasse, near Bogenhausen Park in Munich, and
was just across the Isar River from Hitler's apartment.*

*Below: Adolf Hitler's New Year's card: "Your good wishes for
Christmas and the New Year have pleased me very much.
I return your wishes with heartfelt thanks."*

BERLIN, DEN 1. Januar 1938

ADOLF HITLER

Ihre Glückwünsche zum Weihnachtsfest
und zum Neuen Jahre haben mich sehr erfreut.
Ich erwidere Ihre Wünsche mit herz-
lichem Dank.

ters he took lonely walks around his compound, usually accompanied only by his dog Blondi. He ate alone a great deal, and when he did occasionally invite someone to dine with him he talked only of trivial matters, never about the serious decisions he had to make. Often he would eat in complete silence, not speaking to his guest or the cook. Frau Manzialy, whom he trusted, was a very good cook and liked Hitler. He still had much of his food tasted by others before he would eat, however, since he was afraid his enemies might attempt to poison him. Late in 1943 he told Albert Speer, Nazi Minister of Armaments and Production, "One of these days I'll have only two friends left, Fräulein Braun and my dog."

It was true that he was losing his "friends" very rapidly. On July 25, 1943, Hitler received word that Mussolini had been dismissed by the King of Italy and placed under arrest. This was a profound shock to the Führer. Only six days earlier he had met with the Italian dictator at Feltre in northern Italy, and the two men had expressed their mutual trust and determination to win the war. Hitler felt his prestige was endangered by Mussolini's arrest, because he had constantly referred to Mussolini as the one man to be trusted and had repeatedly stated that the Nazi and Fascist revolutions were the hope of the world. Now his Italian counterpart had suddenly been arrested, forced into an ambulance and taken to a hiding place. Worse yet, no

Eva and Hitler looking at flowers sent to them at the Berghof for a party they hosted.

Italian had fired a shot in protest. Hitler decided he had to make some move to prove to the world that he did not desert his comrades in time of trouble.

"Call Skorzeny to headquarters."

At that time, Otto Skorzeny, a six-foot-four-inch Austrian with a vivid dueling scar across the left side of his face, was the commander of the German Special Forces. A hard drinker and a hard fighter, Skorzeny had never flinched from any assignment, but he was startled the day he met with Hitler at Wolf's Lair (this was the code name for Hitler's headquarters on the Eastern Front) and received his latest orders.

"I cannot and will not leave Italy's greatest son in the lurch," Hitler told Skorzeny. "I will keep faith with my old ally and dear friend. He must be rescued promptly or he will be handed over to the Allies. I herewith order you to carry out a task that is vital for the war."

Hitler did not even tell Eva about this plan for fear it would fail. On the afternoon of September 12, 1943, Skorzeny and his Special Forces used gliders and light planes to rescue Mussolini from a hotel on Gran Sasso, the loftiest peak in the Apennines, one hundred miles from Rome. Skorzeny took the exhausted *Il Duce* to the Hotel Imperial in Vienna, and within an hour Hitler was on the telephone congratulating him. Skorzeny was awarded the Knight's Cross and promoted to Stürmbannführer of the Waffen-SS.

"You have been away from your wife too long, Skorzeny, preparing for this rescue. It is not good for a man to be away from his wife's bed that length of time. Go home and enjoy yourself and make your wife happy," Hitler told him.

Hitler's study and desk, with a photograph of Eva on it; and
Hitler in his typical Führer pose on the wall behind. Eva's desk
at the Berghof is bare by comparison.

Hitler with Eva on his right arm
celebrate the New Year at the Berghof, 1944.

Eva met Skorzeny later when he went to the Berghof, and they became close friends. He spent many hours with her while waiting to see Hitler, both at the Berghof and later in the bunker in Berlin. Eva nodded and smiled when she learned what Hitler had said to Skorzeny about his leave. She said, "He understands. He understands."

Hitler saved face by having Mussolini rescued but not much else. He found the Italian dictator a shrunken, aging, scared man who merely wanted to retire to some quiet place with his mistress Clara Petacci. Disgusted with the change in *Il Duce*, Hitler settled him at Gargnano on Lake Garda and kept him a virtual prisoner. When Mussolini protested that he could not order the execution of his son-in-law, the handsome Count Galeazzo Ciano, who had tried to escape to Spain or Argentina after Italy's fall, Hitler took care of the matter himself. With the calm ruthlessness that had become his trademark, Hitler ordered the death of Ciano in January, 1944. Eva liked the handsome Ciano and had even told Hitler once that he should try to copy the debonair manner of the Italian count, but at the showdown she agreed that he deserved to die. "He arranged his own fate," she told Skorzeny. "He betrayed *Il Duce*, his wife and his children."

The execution of Count Ciano reminded all of those under Hitler that they were utterly in his power. During the long winter of 1943–44 this apprehension was evident wherever Hitler went—Munich, Berlin, Berghof, or Wolf's Lair. No one seemed comfortable with him any longer. Everyone was suspicious of everyone else, as well as afraid of Hitler. It snowed hard for weeks without stopping, during December and January, and walls of snow virtually imprisoned those in the Berghof. Huge amounts had to be shoveled away every day to clear even a narrow path to the teahouse and to open the other entrances and exits.

Eva wanted to go skiing to escape the depressing atmosphere, but Hitler wouldn't give his permission. "You could break a foot," he told her. "It is too dangerous." He became more and more possessive as his troubles mounted. Eva had to be satisfied with long walks along the cleared paths.

While Hitler worried about Eva, she also worried about him. She noticed that his hair was turning much more gray, that he seldom stood straight as he always had during the early years of the Third Reich, that his energy seemed to be waning. One day when she and Traudl Junge were alone, Eva asked, "What do you think about the Führer's health, Frau Junge? I don't want to ask Dr. Morell. I don't trust him and I hate him."

Traudl Junge was diplomatic in her answer. "Fräulein Braun, I know less than you. You know the Führer much better than I do and can deduce things he doesn't tell me."

As though speaking to herself, Eva murmured, "He has become so serious. He worries so much."

"The army reports are enough to make those responsible worry," Frau Junge replied and turned away.

Later that day in the teahouse Eva reproached Hitler. "*Du*, you are so bent over. Can't you straighten up?"

"That comes from carrying such heavy keys in my pocket," he replied. Then, smiling, he added, "Besides, I fit better with you. You wear high heels so you are taller. I bend a little so we fit together very well."

Eva sensed Hitler was mocking her because of her petite size and quickly protested. "I am not short. I am 1.63 meters, like Napoleon."

"How do you know that?" Hitler asked.

Eva wouldn't admit she really didn't know Napoleon's height. "Every educated person knows it."

That evening Hitler was observed checking through the books in the library hunting for statistics on Napoleon's height, but fortunately for Eva he couldn't find any.

Shortly before Christmas, 1943, Fanny Braun visited the Berghof. The Allied bombing raids on Munich and the fact that she hadn't seen Eva for quite some time induced her to make the trip. She rather dreaded the long evening at the Berghof when Hitler talked and talked until the small hours of the morning. She liked her sleep and, in fact, required a great deal of rest, but she also knew Hitler was insulted if anyone left the room before he did. Hitler greeted her with warmth when she arrived at the Berghof, and to her surprise he took her aside that evening and said, "I understand that you need a lot of rest."

Embarrassed and confused, Frau Braun nodded. "*Mein Führer,* I sleep long hours in Munich; that is true."

He took her hand and replied, "I don't want you to mind me, Frau Braun. You go to bed early. I wish that I could sleep for as much as two hours at a stretch."

It was during this visit that Frau Braun first noticed how ill Hitler seemed. Dr. Theodor Morell, his physician, was treating him with injections and pills. At one time during this period he was administering twenty-eight different kinds of medicines to Hitler, many of which gave him more trouble than relief. Morell's penchant for injections was well known and talked about among Hitler's associates, and especially among Hitler's other doctors such as Brandt, Giesing and von Hasselbach. For more than nine years Morell gave the Führer drugs and medications every time he complained about some ailment. If he was tired, Morell stuck a needle in his arm; if he was depressed, the doctor gave him a stimulant; if he couldn't sleep, a sedative; if he had a speech to give, he got a shot before and after the talk. Hitler got a hypodermic needle for every ache and minor complaint involved in the average middle-aged man's existence.

Frau Braun noticed the effects of this therapy during her stay at the Berghof in December, 1943. She told Eva, "The injection helps the Führer for a short time, but when it wears off he is worse than ever."

Eva agreed, but Hitler would not even listen to her warnings concerning Morell, telling her that she did not know anything about medicine and Morell was an expert.

Hitler checks dining table arrangements very carefully.

Below: Despite worsening conditions on all fronts, Hitler took time to share Eva's birthday party at the Berghof in 1944.

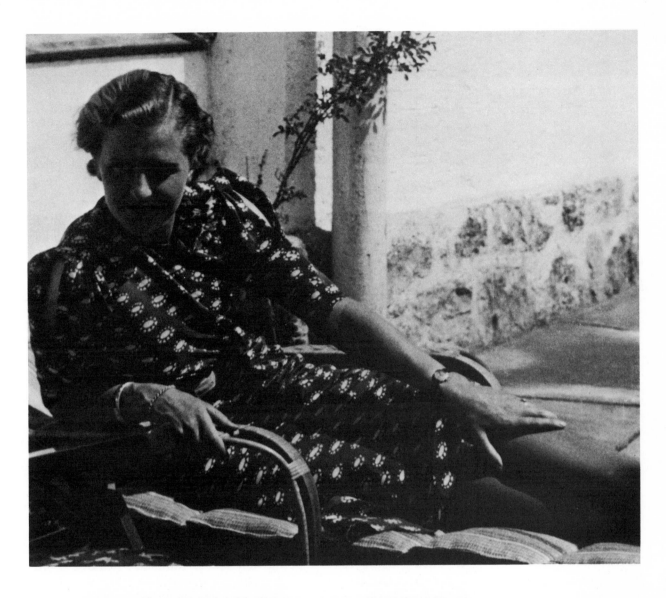

Eva took great pride in her appearance; and a frequent visitor to the Berghof remarked that she never saw Eva in the same dress twice.

A happy group on the Berghof terrace watch Eva's dog Stasi; second and third from right are Albert Speer and Frau Speer.

When Brandt, Giesing and von Hasselbach analyzed one pill that Morell had prescribed for Hitler and discovered that it contained 4.0 milligrams of strychnine and 0.4 milligrams of atropine, they decided that they should tell Hitler the pills were doing him harm. The amounts of both chemicals exceeded the safety level and could have caused a progressive poisoning of the body if taken over a period of time. But when they had given this information to Hitler, he accused them of professional jealousy and lying and had their names removed from his list of attending physicians. Hitler continued to depend on the numerous injections and pills prescribed by Morell.

Eva was also worried about the dangers Hitler faced while at his headquarters in the field. She spent many long hours watching and worrying about the red reflections in the sky over Munich as the Allied bombers attacked the city. Unless it was foggy, the light from the fires could easily be seen from the Berghof. Eva could barely be restrained when the city was being bombed. Hitler had given strict orders that she was not to go to Munich while an air raid was in progress, so she spent hours on the telephone trying to contact friends and her parents in the city. When she did complete a connection she gave instructions about what she wanted done at her villa and asked for an eyewitness account of the bombing. When one of her best friends, the Munich actor Heini Handschuhmacher, was killed during an air raid, she ignored Hitler's orders and with her friend Herta Schneider and her sister Gretl went to the services in Munich. When she returned to the Berghof she was badly shaken by what she had seen in the city—the devastation, the suffering, the dead and injured. Hitler listened to her report on the misery being endured by the population of Munich and vowed that he would pay the Allies back a hundredfold. He also forbade her to go to Munich again while the American and British bombers were in the area.

Another observer of the Allied attacks on Munich was Hermann Fegelein, a young Waffen-SS officer who was noted for his horsemanship, drinking and sexual prowess. He had learned his horsemanship from his father, who operated a riding school in Munich, and the other two talents he developed after joining the Nazis. Tall, slender and a fine dancer (unless he was drunk), Fegelein soon noticed the funloving Gretl Braun at the Berghof. His initial advances were strictly in keeping with his pattern of sexual conquest, but after the ambitious Fegelein gave the matter some thought, he could see many advantages to being married to the sister of Hitler's mistress. His reference to Gretl as "goose" quickly changed to "my love," and by late spring of 1944 he had made up his mind. He proposed. Gretl was fascinated by the dashing SS officer who wore such gaudy uniforms and was so popular among the unmarried—and married—women at the Berghof. She asked her mother's advice about marrying Fegelein but her mother shook her head. "I know nothing about him."

Gretl reminded Fanny Braun that she had met him at the Berghof, but her mother couldn't place the man. The following day

Whenever Eva traveled, she always stayed at the best hotels, dined in the best restaurants, and shopped at the best stores. Here, second from left, she is outside the Bayerrischer Hof in Munich with friends.

Herta Ostermyer (her married name was Schneider), Eva's closest friend, to whom she revealed many facts of her life with Adolf Hitler.

Above: Eva in Innsbruck with Ilse and friends during a vacation trip.

Actress-director Leni Riefenstahl (left) was often seen with Hitler and rumors circulated that they were in love. But, despite the fact that Leni was one of Hitler's intimate companions, Eva's relationship with Hitler was never in danger.

Eva enjoyed taking photos and was frequently seen either with a still camera or, as here, with a movie camera "shooting" her favorite subject.

Fegelein showed up in person at the Braun household and asked Fritz' and Fanny Braun's consent to marry Gretl. Hitler, he said, was delighted with the match, as was Eva. Taking him at his word, the Brauns finally consented to the marriage, which took place on June 3, 1944.

The ceremony was held in the Salzburg town hall. Eva, as soon as she learned of her sister's wedding plans, had the entire staff of Heyse fashion salon in Berlin come to the Berghof to make the wedding dresses. She also convinced Hitler to permit Gretl to have the wedding reception in the Eagle's Nest. It seemed that since Eva herself could not have an elaborate wedding, she intended to lavish all her attention on her sister's. She persuaded Hitler to allow

dancing at the reception, one of the few times he permitted dancing at an affair on the Obersalzberg during the war. She hired a band and made certain there was plenty to drink and eat. For this one night the death and destruction outside the windows of the Eagle's Nest were forgotten. Even the hated Bormann (one of the most powerful and ruthless men in Hitler's inner circle

Count Ciano, Mussolini's son-in-law, at a meeting with Hitler when they were on good terms. Hitler later ordered his execution when it was believed Ciano was trying to escape to South America.

who had always hated Eva and had frequently tried to poison Hitler's mind against her) forgot his ambitions for a few hours and drank so much champagne that

Hitler appears almost "fatherly"
shown (here, and pages 92 and 93),
with Uschi, the baby girl many
believed to be his and Eva's child.
Investigation indicated that Uschi
was Herta Schneider s, Eva's close
friend's daughter. Below, Eva and
Sepp Dietrich enjoying their lapful
of children at the Berghof.

Again, Hitler shown in unlikely company; while (below) Eva helps Uschi walk down the steps at the Berghof.

he had to be carried back to his quarters. Hitler attended the reception but left early. The others, however—including Eva—stayed until dawn dancing, drinking and forgetting.

Three days later—on June 6, 1944—the Allies invaded Europe. Hitler, who was still sleeping when the Normandy invasion was reported to the Berghof, was awakened and told the news. He was so excited that he leaped out of bed and started running out of the room. Eva stopped him.

"*Du*, on this important day it would not be right for the greatest man in the world to be seen wearing only his nightclothes."

Curiously, Hitler seemed more relieved than worried once the Allied invasion had begun. He had been expecting it for so long, wondering where the Americans and British would land on the coast of France. Now that the enemy troops were actually on the soil of Europe, Hitler juggled his available divisions around like chess figures. He didn't trust his generals and constantly intervened and changed their battle plans. By the end of June both the Russians in the east and the joint American-British forces in the west were making sizable advances against the German ground troops—due, in large measure, to Hitler's inept handling of the German military forces. On July 1, 1944, Hitler decided he needed a rest from the forward headquarters where he had been staying since the invasion and returned to the Berghof.

He was very depressed during the first two weeks of July. Eva tried to cheer him up but was only partially successful. During a late dinner with Christa Schröder, a secretary, Hitler said, "I feel something is in the air."

Fräulein Schröder was puzzled. "What do you mean, *mein Führer?*"

"I am afraid something is going to happen to me, and there is no one else who can take over the leadership."

The secretary, always outspoken and never afraid of Hitler, asked, "Do you not have a successor in mind?"

"Hess is gone. He was insane. Göring wouldn't have the sympathy of the people. Himmler is a completely nonartistic person," Hitler said, dismissing the most obvious choices.

"But, *mein Führer*, being an artist is not necessary for a person to be Chancellor," the secretary said. "One can always engage capable people."

Hitler frowned. "It is not so simple to engage capable people, Fräulein. If it were, I would have already hired them."

"Who else do you have in mind as a successor then? Himmler is most often named by the people."

Hitler became very angry with his secretary when she mentioned Himmler's name a second time. "Don't worry your head any further about who should be my successor."

It was obvious to Fräulien Schröder that he was insulted that anyone would think he would be succeeded by Himmler—or anyone else. She quickly changed the subject.

At the moment Hitler and Fräulein

A rare photo of Adolf Hitler, smiling! Associates said Eva made him smile more often than anyone else.

Schröder were talking, a group of German army officers was putting the finishing touches on an assassination plan that they thought near-perfect. Count Klaus von Stauffenberg, a thirty-six-year-old colonel who had been wounded in action several times during World War II, decided that he would kill Hitler or die in the attempt. Aided by a small group of fellow officers, Stauffenberg put a bomb in his briefcase with a report he had to give to Hitler and headed for the Führer's field headquarters in East Prussia. His co-conspirators were strategically placed in Berlin and elsewhere in Germany, awaiting word that Hitler was dead so they could take control of their assigned areas.

As the conference was getting underway at the field headquarters— at 12:30 P.M. on July 20, 1944—Eva and her friend Herta Schneider were swimming in the Königsee, near Berchtesgaden. It was a hot day; the sun was just right for getting a tan and for sleeping. Eva was on a raft several hundred feet from shore, resting before starting her swim back, when she noticed a car approaching from the direction of the Berghof. She knew immediately by the speed of the car that something was wrong. Diving into the waters of the Königsee, she swam as fast as she could toward the shore.

A short time before, Stauffenberg had entered the conference room, spoken to Hitler and then placed the deadly briefcase against a table leg near the Führer. The fuse mechanism had already been activated. Less than a minute later, the would-be assassin left the room on the pretext of having to telephone Berlin . . . and kept on going

toward his parked airplane. He had not yet reached the aircraft when the bomb exploded. Through the dust and smoke, Hitler walked out of the shattered conference room. His clothes were ripped, his hair was partially burned away, his right arm hung useless at his side and he had a multitude of bruises.

The message Eva received from the chauffeur of the car that arrived at the Königsee that afternoon was, "There was an attempt on the Führer's life but he wants you to know that he is all right."

Eva hurried back to the Berghof and desperately tried to reach Hitler by telephone but failed. By the time Hitler finally contacted her she was nearly hysterical, certain that he was badly hurt or dead. His voice reassured her that the assassination attempt had failed. When she saw his blood-stained uniform several days after the explosion, however, she nearly went into hysterics again.

"Only a miracle saved you," she cried, holding his arm tightly.

It was then that Hitler repeated one of his most quoted phrases:

> *I consider that it is by the grace of Providence that I have been chosen to lead my people in such a war. After my miraculous escape from death I am more than ever convinced that it is my fate to bring this war to a successful conclusion.*

The Providence that Hitler alluded to was certainly kind to him that day. Of the twenty-four men in the room when the bomb exploded four died, three others were injured seriously and the remainder were shaken and bruised.

Christa Schröder, who was at the field headquarters with Hitler, went to her room to compose herself after hearing of the attempt on Hitler's life that July afternoon. She wondered when she would see him again and what he would look like when she did. She was still worrying about his injuries when she was startled by the adjutant who walked into her room.

"The Führer requests your presence at dinner," Schaub said.

The secretary looked at him in amazement. "The Führer can walk?"

"The Führer will eat at 3 P.M."

When she arrived at the dining room she was astonished to see how fresh and lively Hitler appeared. He greeted her in the same polite manner he always used with his secretaries and waited until she was seated before he sat down. He described to her the way his aides had reacted to the assassination attempt. Linge, he said, had been furious and Arndt had cried. He stared at her, recalling his earlier conversation about a successor, and said, "Believe me, this is a turning point for Germany. Now it will go uphill again. I am happy that the *Schweinehunde* have unmasked themselves."

The secretary was aware that Mussolini was scheduled to meet with Hitler that afternoon, but she assumed that the meeting had been canceled because of the attempt on the Führer's life.

"On the contrary," Hitler said. "I must receive him. What would the world press write if I didn't receive him?"

Hitler took Mussolini to the wrecked conference room and explained what had happened. Mussolini echoed the Führer's comments about his narrow escape from death. "After what I have seen here, I am absolutely of your opinion. This was a sign from Heaven."

Heavenly solicitation apparently did not extend to Hitler's health. Eva saw him only periodically during the four months after the assassination attempt, since he remained at the East Prussian headquarters. On each of his rare visits with her, however, his physical deterioration was more marked. His hands shook, especially his left; his ears bothered him very badly and an examination showed that the tympanic membranes on both sides were broken; the on-and-off stomach cramps that had bothered him for years now became a constant nagging pain; and his head ached continually. Between the effects of the bomb and Morell's injections he was in very bad shape. In September Eva was notified that he was sick in bed, and she was terrified.

"He has never been in that condition since I have known him," she told Gretl. "What shall I do?"

Hitler would not permit Eva to visit his field headquarters; the area was too dangerous. There was nothing she could do but stay either in Munich or on the Obersalzberg and wait for word. He telephoned her every evening, but even the sound of his voice was not reassuring. He talked more slowly, his voice husky. In October

Eva was told that the doctors had discovered a polyp on his vocal cords and they had operated. After that, she could not even depend on his nightly telephone calls, and it was not until November 20, 1944, when Hitler left the Wolf's Lair for the last time and went to Berlin, that she was able to see him.

Eva was shocked at his appearance. He looked many years older than he had in early July. His face had the blue-gray appearance of death, he shuffled instead of walked and his hands shook much worse than before. He saw her staring and said, "It is better that my hands shake than my head."

Hitler discovered upon his return that Berlin had been badly damaged by the enemy, too. A large part of the Reich Chancellery had been destroyed by the Allied bombs, and the surrounding area was a mass of rubble. By a quirk of fate his private quarters in the Reich Chancellery building were not damaged, and he and Eva spent their days and nights there until December 10, 1944, when Hitler departed for Adlerhorst, his field headquarters in the west. Eva pleaded with him not to go, insisting that he could conduct the war from Berlin just as well, but Hitler refused. "I must be in personal contact with my generals," he said. "They will no longer do what I order unless I am with them."

When Eva scolded him, saying that his health was more important to her than another victory on the battlefield, he stared at her for a long time before he answered. "You are the only one who would say that. You are the only one who cares." This—one of the most affectionate remarks he ever made to her in public—was true. By now Hitler was undoubtedly the most hated man in the world.

Germany was losing the war. Unless the German army could reverse the situation soon, the Führer, the inner circle, the country, were doomed. Hitler's entourage pressed him for a winning strategy, a dazzling new plan that would bring Germany victory and save their lives and careers. Only Eva was concerned for Adolf Hitler personally.

The closest the German military forces came to reversing the tide was their counteroffensive in the Ardennes Forest—the Battle of the Bulge—but that, too, ended in defeat. With the Russian forces pushing him from the east in a new concerted drive to reach Berlin, and the Western armies headed full speed toward the Rhine from the west, Hitler decided to return to Berlin for his final stand. He moved into his private quarters in the Reich Chancellery, and during the Allied bombing raids he spent hours in the bunker underneath the building. When Eva received a telephone call from him informing her that he was there, she quickly went to Berlin from her villa in Munich.

"This time you will stay with me," she told Hitler when he greeted her in his second-floor quarters. "I will take care of you. We will not part again."

Late in January, Eva's sister Ilse arrived in Berlin. She had been forced to flee from Breslau ahead of the advancing Allied ground troops. Eva arranged for her to stay at the Hotel Adlon, still intact, and invited

Above: The magnificent scenery of the Berghof is clearly evident in the photo of Hitler's aides walking to the teahouse, one of his favorite places.

Below: A Hitler convoy approaching the outer perimeter of the Berghof, with Eva trying to catch all the sun she can by standing in the car.

her to dinner at the Reich Chancellery. The two sisters were friendly, but Eva knew that Ilse still disliked Hitler. When Ilse criticized the destruction of Germany, blaming the catastrophe on Hitler, they had an argument, but later that evening when they parted, Eva kissed her sister. "Everything will be all right."

They never saw one another again.

On February 8, 1945, Hitler sent Eva to the Berghof on the pretext that she must get everything ready there in case he decided to move his staff to the Obersalzberg later. At first Eva was reluctant to leave Berlin and Hitler, but she suddenly changed her mind. She took her two dogs and many of her personal possessions, such as jewelry and photo albums, with her. Gretl, pregnant, accompanied her. Instead of going to the Berghof, however, Eva stopped at Munich. Gretl continued on to the Berghof to stay until the military situation was resolved and her husband—who was in Berlin with Hitler as Himmler's representative—could join her.

In Munich, Eva put her villa in order, arranged for friends to care for her dogs and visited her parents. She also made a special trip through the rubble-strewn streets to spend an afternoon with her close friend Herta Schneider and her children, whom Eva loved very much. She was more affectionate than usual with the children, and when she left the Schneider home she kissed Herta. "We have had such lovely times together."

Herta nodded. "I will meet you at the Berghof in a few days and we will go boating again. The bombers will not bother us there."

Eva smiled but said nothing. Later that day Fanny Braun told Eva that if the Allied bombers continued to attack Munich, she would join her on the Obersalzberg, too. She noticed that Eva seemed more quiet than usual and that her farewell kiss was exceptionally long, but she thought it was because Eva was tired and depressed.

"A stay at the Berghof will cheer you up," she told her daughter.

Eva nodded but made no reply. She didn't want her mother or her father or Herta or Gretl or anyone else to know that she had no intention of continuing south to the Berghof. She was going back to Berlin and Hitler.

Eva at the Königsee. She was here, swimming, when the attempt on Hitler's life was made at the Wolf's Lair, his headquarters on the eastern front, on July 20, 1944.

7. For Better or for Worse

The cruelty of Adolf Hitler was never more evident than during the last weeks of the Third Reich. He was vicious and vindictive to the end . . . except with Eva Braun.

Once Eva determined to return to Berlin, she made the arrangements quickly. Since Hitler did not know she was returning and she did not want to alert him for fear he would try to stop her, Eva did not dare to ask him to send his plane for her. Flying wasn't safe anyway because the sky was filled with Allied aircraft. A lone Luftwaffe airplane would be easy prey. She finally talked a young Waffen-SS officer, Walther Galen, into driving her to Berlin in her Mercedes-Benz.

It was a dangerous trip. The American 8th Air Force and 15th Air Force and the British Royal Air Force were out in full strength during March when Eva made her trip. On March 14, 1945, the day she left Munich, 1,246 heavy bombers of the 8th Air Force attacked high-priority targets all over Germany. Near Leipzig two Mustang fighters accompanying the bombers actually made a strafing run on Eva's automobile, but Galen saw them coming and managed to park under a viaduct. One tire was blown apart but there was a spare in the trunk, and within an hour Eva was on her way north again. Another strafing attack outside Dessau startled her. An American P-38 pilot blew up a German army truck

Eva's fondness for animals never waned; here, on the Obersalzberg, she sits on a placid cow's back.

Above: Adolf Hitler, ordinary citizen, reading at breakfast.

Left: Eva with Stasi (Negus is just a shadow at the end of the leash), and Hitler with his beloved Blondi—he had her and her pups poisoned in the Berlin bunker, just before the end.

Eva, clowning, standing in high heels on the spare tire of her Mercedes, with an equally fun-loving friend.

that Galen had been following on the highway. The Waffen-SS officer decided to stop in a nearby wood and wait until dark before traveling any farther. He and Eva were both weary and fell asleep. When they awoke it was nearly three o'clock in the morning, much later than Galen had planned to continue the trip.

At about the same time that Eva and her driver headed north again, the heavy-bomber crews of the 8th Air Force were huddled in their briefing rooms in England, looking at their maps for the next day's missions. The chief target for the day was the headquarters of the German high command at Zossen, twenty-eight miles from Berlin—almost directly in the path of Eva's Mercedes-Benz. Unaware of the armada of Allied bombers heading in her direction, Eva was relaxing in the rear seat of the automobile as Galen neared Berlin. Suddenly she sat up with a jerk as he brought the Mercedes-Benz to a stop.

"Get out and run for the shelter!"

Eva didn't hesitate. She opened the door of the automobile and raced toward the public shelter a few yards to her right. Just as she entered it the first of the bombs exploded to the west. The 8th Air Force Liberators and Flying Fortresses dropped 1,400 tons of high explosives in the vicinity of Berlin that day (March 15, 1944), but Eva was about ten miles away from Zossen, their main objective, and in all probability this saved her life.

After the Allied bombers had left the Zossen area on their way back to England, Eva and Galen drove the remaining distance into Berlin. She was stunned when she saw the city. The Reich Chancellery—which they had to approach by using the road through the gateway of the old Zossen Palace because the other streets were pitted with bomb craters—was in much worse condition than when she had left Berlin. There were huge holes blasted in all four sides of the building. The American Embassy was demolished; the city post office was badly damaged. Unter den Linden, the promenade she loved and where she had spent so many hours walking while waiting for Hitler, was practically obliterated. Tree trunks were scattered across it; bomb craters filled with water made it an obstacle course for any pedestrian brave enough to try and walk across it; and along one side there were sandbags piled high by German soldiers who hoped to hide behind them when the Russians arrived. The only trouble was that the soldiers, mostly teenage boys, didn't know from which direction the Soviet troops would enter the city.

Eva went directly to Hitler's study in his private quarters of the Reich Chancellery, which—despite the mounting damage to the structure—was still intact. Hitler was sitting on the blue-and-white patterned sofa when she entered the room, and for a moment he just stared at her. Putting his trembling hands on the arms of the sofa, he pushed himself to his feet and came toward her.

"I told you to go to the Berghof."

Despite Hitler's angry tone, it was obvious to everyone who witnessed the reunion—the secretaries, Schaub and Magda Goebbels—that he was pleased to see Eva. When she took his hands in hers he smiled and motioned for her to sit down on the sofa. They sat there for most of the evening, talking about earlier days, looking at photograph albums, listening to records. When Eva left the room to wash up after her long and hazardous trip, Hitler bragged to his secretaries about her loyalty.

"Who else would come back to Berlin when they had the opportunity to go to the Berghof?" he asked several times.

The secretaries did not answer and Hitler did not press them. He knew very well that many of those in Berlin that night wished they were on the Obersalzberg, miles away from the attacking bombers and the advancing Russian soldiers. He himself still had tentative plans to make his last stand in the mountains near the Berghof.

During the remainder of March, Hitler assured Eva that the city would not fall, that foreign troops had not marched into Berlin since 1806 and it would not happen again in 1945. She heard rumors that disturbed her, however, just as the appearance of the city had disturbed her on her return. It was said that the Americans had crossed the Rhine over the bridge at Remagen, and that the Soviet troops were closing in on Vienna and threatening to cross the Oder River. Despite this depressing news, Eva rarely took refuge in the thirty-room bunker fifty feet beneath the Reich Chancellery, except during the last week of March when the attacks became more intense.

The bunker had two floors. Eva's and Hitler's quarters were on the lower floor, which was much more plush than the one above. The upper floor was used primarily for a kitchen, servants' quarters and guest accommodations. Eva lacked little in the way of comfort except, of course, the opportunity to see the sun and stars. Her quarters were air-conditioned and carpeted and included a private bath and monogrammed furniture. She had a dressing room and a combination bedroom-sitting room, both of which were accessible from Hitler's study. Hitler's bedroom was on the opposite side of the study, and beyond it was a map-conference room and a speical room for Blondi, his dog. The study, where he and Eva spent many hours during the final days of the Third Reich, had a writing table, a couch, a small table and several upholstered chairs. There was a private vestibule off the main corridor that led to Eva's and Hitler's quarters.

Most of the time Eva remained in her own quarters or in Hitler's. The depressing atmosphere in the underground headquarters did not deter Eva from maintaining her appearance, even as the military situation worsened. She applied makeup carefully, kept her fingernails well manicured and wore a different dress as often as possible. She even managed to smuggle in hairdressers among the multitude of officers, ministers and their wives and other visitors who came to the bunker during late March and early April. She not only tried to look her best, she also acted her best. While others were morbid, quiet, pessimistic—and with reason—Eva continually tried to establish a more lighthearted atmosphere around Hitler. She knew time was running out, but she never gave up trying.

On April 1, 1945, she was in her combination bedroom-sitting room when Schaub announced she had a guest. A moment later Heinrich Hoffmann entered the room.

"Heinrich!"

They embraced in silence for several seconds. Eva had not seen Hoffmann for six months, not since Morell and Bormann had convinced Hitler the photographer had paratyphus and his presence would endanger the health of the Führer.

"Have you seen the Führer?" Eva asked.

Hoffmann shook his head. "Not yet. I have fifty documents with me proving that I never had paratyphus, but when I tried to show them to the Führer he backed away from me and would not talk with me." There were tears in the photographer's eyes as he looked at Eva. "I, the Führer's closest friend, can't even talk with him."

Eva motioned for him to sit down. "I will talk with the Führer."

She disappeared into Hitler's study and was gone for several minutes. When she returned she was smiling.

"We will have tea with the Führer at three o'clock. There is just one condition—do not mention your supposed illness."

Hoffmann updated Eva on the news from Munich, including the information that her mother was well and that her father was on duty at a military hospital in the Munich area. He told her that he had heard Gretl was getting bigger every day while she awaited the birth of her baby at the Berghof, but he had no news about Ilse. By the time the adjutant arrived to tell them Hitler was waiting for them in his study, Eva was in a better humor than she had been for days.

Hoffmann and Hitler talked as though there had not been a six-month hiatus in their relationship. While Eva listened, the two men talked about the paintings Hitler still wanted for his collection, Hitler's favorite photographs—everything but Hoffmann's supposed illness and the military situation. Eva was delighted in the change that came over Hitler as he joked with the photographer about Hoffmann's added weight since the last time he had seen him, about his love of liquor and women and his large inventory of obscene stories. She later told Frau Junge that she had not seen the Führer "in such good spirits since his days at the Berghof during the early part of the war." Hitler, the teetotaler, even insisted that Hoffmann have several drinks after they had finished their tea. When it came time to part, at five o'clock on the morning of April 2, Hitler solemnly shook hands with his longtime friend from Munich, gripping Hoffmann's hand for several long moments. Then, without a word, he abruptly turned and walked back into his bedroom.

Hoffmann stayed a few minutes longer with Eva, long enough to ask her if she wanted to accompany him back to Munich. Eva shook her head.

"I will stay with the Führer."

The rotund photographer shrugged. He

Eva and Albert Speer, enjoying "the better days."

*Above and right: A movie
company made film on the
Obersalzberg, but a print of it has
never been found since World War
II. Eva is shown with the film
crew, taking photographs.*

*Hitler (far right) and Eva, preoccupied with
hosting a children's birthday party at the
Berghof.*

was an ardent Nazi and considered himself one of Hitler's closest friends, but he had no intention of staying in Berlin until it was too late to get out.

"I'll see you later," he told Eva as he kissed her on the cheek.

Eva smiled. "Perhaps."

One of the brightest events in the bunker during April was the arrival of news that Franklin D. Roosevelt had died. But the excitement didn't last long; no one really thought the death of one Allied leader could change the course of the war. It did give Hitler a few cheerful hours contemplating the historical parallel with the death of the Czarina Elizabeth of Russia at a crucial moment, which saved the kingdom of Frederick the Great. Eva, more realistic, was interested in Hitler's upcoming birthday. On April 20 he would be fifty-six years old and she wanted to celebrate the event. She was worried, however. The Führer was losing his temper more often as the days passed, going into a tantrum at the slightest provocation. He constantly screamed at General Hans Krebbs, the new Army Chief of Staff; General Wilhelm Burgdorf, the army adjutant; General Karl Koller, the Chief of Staff of the Luftwaffe; and Heinz Lorenz, from the Ministry of Propaganda. He even had a three-hour verbal battle with General Heinz Guderian during which he bellowed so much that his voice became hoarse and his throat sore. Often he was insulting to the secretaries, and Eva had to try and smooth things over after he left the room. She sensed that his lack of control was hurting his image as a strong leader, that the loyal officers and others in the bunker were losing their remaining respect for him. That is why she wanted to stage a birthday celebration in his honor, to establish him once again as the "Great One."

A birthday party in an underground bunker, in the midst of the brutal bombardment of a city and country, was no easy thing to arrange. But Eva was so intent on giving Hitler some pleasure on his birthday that she never considered how grotesque this affair was bound to be. She invited all the Nazi leaders, and for the last time Speer, Goebbels, Bormann, Göring, Himmler, Ribbentrop and many lesser Nazi officers were gathered together. Their presents were not so lavish as in past years, but Hitler did receive two gifts that he appreciated. One was a painting of his mother, the other a portrait of Eva in a jeweled frame. He put them both in his study so that he could see them several times a day as he passed through the room. As the guests greeted him and wished him good fortune in the future, Hitler tried to conceal his physical infirmities. He braced himself against the couch in order to reduce the shaking of his body, but he couldn't control his hands; they shook as though he had palsy. Eva stood beside him and tried to divert the guests' attention from the Führer as they greeted him, but she was only partially successful. Their shock at seeing his physical condition was mirrored in their expressions.

Hitler left the party early and Eva accompanied him to his quarters. She was disappointed that her party had turned out so badly. Hitler was melancholy and brooding, so dejected he had not even noticed the new dress of silver-blue brocade Eva had saved for the occasion. So far she had escaped being the target of his anger, but she was not confident that she would escape much longer. In fact, she was not confident of anything now that Hitler no longer seemed to believe he would ultimately be victorious. On a sudden impulse Eva decided to have one last fling, to enjoy herself once more as she had in the earlier days in Munich at the *Oktoberfest* when she danced, drank and sang all night.

After returning to the party from Hitler's quarters Eva suggested to the guests that they go up to the Führer's apartment—or what was left of it—in the Reich Chancellery and continue the affair. The living room of the apartment was still intact but bare since the furniture had been moved into the bunker. Only a large round table remained, standing in the center of the room. At first the guests were reluctant to leave the safety of the bunker, even though there was no Allied air raid in progress. Eva and several of the younger Waffen-SS officers went up the steps alone, carrying a phonograph with them and a supply of food and drink. Within a few minutes the others followed, lured by the opportunity to get out of the "concrete prison" for a few hours and forget the approaching disaster with wine, women and song. Morell, nervous and dejected because Hitler had accused him of trying to inject him with morphine, followed Eva. So did Bormann, afraid of missing some remarks or gossip he could relay to Hitler. Traudl Junge went because she, too, wanted one last fling. Soon most of the guests were crowded into the

room in the Chancellery, dancing to the single record Eva had brought along for the phonograph, a record that repeated over and over that "blood red roses tell you of happiness . . ."

Eva danced with everyone that night. Between dances she and the guests drank champagne, and as the night went on a giddiness came over all of them. Their shrill laughter echoed in the room, passing through the holes in the Chancellery walls and drifting into the blacked-out streets of Berlin. Once in a while, when an artillery shell burst in the city, the guests would be quiet for a moment—but only for a moment—and then the laughter and talking would resume. No one spoke about the war, or of victory or defeat. They just danced, drank champagne, laughed and listened to the record chant on and on. Not until the sun came up on the morning of April 21, 1945 did Eva and her guests leave the damaged Reich Chancellery building and retreat down the steps into the bunker. The party was over.

Eva knew there had been a conference between Hitler and his officers after his birthday reception, but it wasn't until the next day that she heard of Hitler's decision to stay—and, if necessary, die—in Berlin. She had thought he was going to move to the Obersalzberg, and that the German army would make its last stand in that mountainous area. When she awakened early in the afternoon, however, she discovered that a mass exit from the bunker was in progress. Göring, in fact, had begun the procession to the Berghof late the night before. Hitler had bid him an abrupt, cold

Hitler, stopping to chat with
an associate, on the
Obersalzberg.

Eva enjoying herself
at a Nazi rally.

With Hitler and friends on the hillside above the Berghof.

Hitler, wearing civilian clothes, leaving the Berghof with an associate. Eva can be seen on the right, partially obscured.

farewell, not mentioning their long years of association or the great victories they had once shared. The Führer was angry with Göring because his Luftwaffe had failed to protect Germany from the Allied bombers; he was glad to see "the fat one" go. Albert Speer also left Berlin, after trying to convince Hitler not to order a "scorched earth" policy for what remained of Germany. Eva hated to see Speer go and was especially disappointed that she had not had the opportunity to bid him farewell. Himmler departed for his quarters at Ziethen Castle, not mentioning to Hitler his personal plans to end the war through negotiations with Count Folke Bernadotte of Sweden. Ribbentrop was preparing to leave the bunker when Eva awakened. Before he left, he stopped to see her.

"You are the only one who can take the Führer away from here," he told Eva. "Tell him that you want to leave Berlin with him. You can thereby do Germany a great service."

Although she was shocked that Hitler intended to stay in the bunker until the end, she didn't intend to reveal her emotions to Ribbentrop.

"I will not tell the Führer anything," she replied. "He must decide alone. If he thinks it is right to stay in Berlin then I will stay with him. If he goes, I go, too."

Ribbentrop kissed Eva on the cheek and left, shaking his head in frustration.

Others also left the bunker that day while the roads were still open and escape was possible. Fräulein Wolfe, Hitler's long-time secretary, and Christa Schröder both departed, as did Morell, the deposed physi-

cian. Many of the staff officers rushed to head south before the Russians arrived.

Later that afternoon Hitler met with his two remaining secretaries, Traudl Junge and Gerda Daranowski (who had married General Eckhardt Christian a few months earlier), Fräulein Manzialy (his favorite cook) and Eva. He announced that within the hour an airplane would arrive in Berlin to fly them out of the city to the Berghof.

"All is lost, hopelessly lost," Hitler told the four women. "It is best you go to the Obersalzberg immediately."

He turned to leave the room but Eva quickly went to his side and took both his hands in hers. As though speaking to a child, she said, "But you know I will stay with you. I won't leave."

At that moment Hitler leaned over and kissed Eva on the lips, the first time any of those present had seen him do such a thing in all the years they had known him. The two secretaries and the cook then told him that they, too, intended to stay.

At dinner that evening Hitler gave each of the women a small cylinder that resembled an ornate lipstick holder. Opening one, he slipped a small phial from it into his hand. Indicating the golden-colored liquid in the phial, Hitler said, "This is potassium cyanide. There is enough in the phial to kill a man or woman. I suggest you keep it with you from now on to use if and when you want to do so."

This was his way of warning them that they might prefer death by poison to the treatment they could expect from the Russian soldiers if captured alive.

Once she had made the decision to stay

and die in Berlin with Hitler, Eva did not isolate herself in her quarters and brood. She was determined "to act like a lady until the end." She set two goals for herself: to keep Hitler as happy as possible under the circumstances, and to make all necessary preparations for the end. No longer could she hope to become the official "First Lady" of Germany; she knew Hitler would not have any country to rule within a few days. All her personal objectives, which in earlier years had seemed so important, were now forgotten. She thought only of Hitler—and of her parents and sisters.

She admitted to Speer, when he made his dramatic flight back to Berlin on April 23 to visit Hitler one final time, that her most difficult task was retaining her self-control.

"One needs courage when death is near. I hope that my courage does not fail me in the end," she said when Speer visited her in the bunker while waiting to see Hitler. Suddenly she brightened. "How about some champagne for a farewell drink? And some food? You must be hungry after your flight."

Speer had seen many others in the bunker that night—Goebbels and his wife, Bormann, various generals—but in his eyes only Eva was composed and calm. The others were either drunk, drugged or in a stupor because of their fear of approaching death. When it came time for him to leave, Eva made one last parting remark: "Why does the killing continue? It's all for nothing." She was the only one in the bunker who mentioned the suffering of others.

Whenever it was possible during the final weeks of the battle for Berlin, Eva slipped out of the bunker to walk in the Reich Chancellery garden. She had always loved the springtime, the mild air, the warm sun—but in April, 1945, there were deep holes in the new grass where the Russian artillery shells had landed, and empty ammunition cans, bottles, broken tree limbs and crushed flowers were everywhere. Several times she was forced to run for shelter when the Russian shells landed nearby, and finally on April 25 she decided that it was not safe to go outside the bunker any more.

In the midst of the general despair and destruction Eva remained composed. When Göring sent a message by radio that he took it for granted the Führer expected him to assume "total leadership of the Third Reich," Hitler went into a rage and ordered his arrest. Eva managed to calm him during a conversation later in his study. While the others present listened in silence she diverted his mind from the Göring affair.

"Do you remember that statue in the Foreign Office garden?" she asked Hitler. "It would look wonderful standing beside the pool in the garden of my Munich villa. Please buy it for me after we leave Berlin."

Surprisingly, Hitler gave the ridiculous request serious consideration. "But I don't know to whom it belongs. It is probably state property. I couldn't just take it and say you could put it in your private garden if it is state property."

Eva laid her hand on his arm and replied, "Oh, if you succeed in beating back the Russians and freeing Berlin, then you can make an exception."

Hitler gave a short laugh and muttered, more to himself than to the others in the room, "The logic of women!"

Later in the evening when he once again began ranting about the "traitorous Göring," Eva changed the subject to other matters. She walked over to him and pointed to several red and blue spots on Hitler's gray field uniform coat.

"Look, you are quite dirty. You mustn't do everything like old Fritz (Frederick the Great) and run around as unkempt as he."

Hitler, diverted, protested mildy. "But this is my work suit. I can't put on an apron when I go to a conference and have to handle colored pencils."

During this last week Eva showed the same quiet composure and muted cheerfulness that she had exhibited during most of her association with Hitler. Hanna Reitsch, the famous German aviatrix, saw Eva when she flew General Ritter von Greim to the bunker on April 26 after Hitler had appointed Greim to replace Göring. Eva was by far the calmest of the bunker occupants,

One of the final photos taken of Eva and Adolf Hitler at the Berghof. Notice Hitler is using a cane. Shortly after, Hitler left the Obersalzberg and went to Berlin to make his final stand; and Eva joined him there a few weeks later, to die with him in the bunker.

much more composed than Frau Goebbels. Fräulein Reitsch noticed that when Eva was in Hitler's presence she was always charming and thoughtful of his every comfort, well-dressed and as attractive as possible under the circumstances. She seemed to take the prospect of dying with Hitler quite matter-of-factly, with an attitude that seemed to say, "Has not our relationship been of many long years' duration, and did I not try to commit suicide when he wanted to get rid of me? This will be much easier and more proper."

When Reitsch and Greim flew out of Berlin at Hitler's orders between midnight and 1 A.M. on April 29, Fräulein Reitsch carried a letter that Eva had written to her sister Gretl. The letter was never delivered, but Reitsch recalled that it stated:

I must write you these words so that you will not feel sad over our end here in the shelter. It is rather we who are filled with sorrow because it is your fate to live on into the chaos that will follow. For myself I am glad to die here; glad to die at the side of the Führer; but most of all glad that the horror now to come is spared me. What could life still give me? It has already been perfect. It has already given me its best and its fullest. Why should I go on living? This is the time to die; the right time. With the Führer I have had everything. To die now, beside him, completes my happiness. Live on as well and as happily as you can. Shed no tears nor be regretful over our deaths. It is the perfect and proper ending. None of us would change it now. It is the right end for a German woman.

8. "Until Death Do Us Part"

Hitler often said: "There are two ways of judging a man's character: by the woman he marries and by the way he dies." In late April, 1945, it was time for Adolf Hitler to do both.

On April 25, while Eva stood nearby listening, Hitler gave precise instructions to his valet, Heinz Linge, about destroying all his personal effects after his death except for the Graff portrait of Frederick the Great—Hans Baur, his personal pilot, would fly it out of Berlin.

Everything else—papers, letters, photographs, official documents—was to be burned. When he went into detail about how he intended to shoot himself after taking poison and how he wanted his body burned, Eva, still dry-eyed but shaken, turned and walked out of the room. She intended to die with him, but she did not want to talk about death. Later, however, she told Frau Junge, "I want to be a pretty corpse. I'm going to take poison." She took the brass tube with the phial of cyanide out of the pocket of her elegant dress and examined it carefully. "I wonder whether it hurts. I am so afraid of having to suffer for a long time."

The secretary tried to cheer Eva up by saying that Hitler had promised her there would be no pain, but she hurriedly excused herself and went to her own room.

Eva wearing the silver fox fur coat which she offered to Traudl Junge just before Eva and Hitler committed suicide.

Both Frau Junge and Fräulein Manzialy had decided to try to escape from Berlin after Hitler's death rather than commit suicide. Later Gerda Christian joined in the plan. They intended to remain loyal to Hitler as long as he was alive but agreed that once he was dead their obligation to him was over. Whether they could get out of the inferno alive or not was doubtful.

Eva never doubted that she would die when Hitler died, but the suspense was hard on her nerves. Every time the news about the military situation was bad, Hitler muttered that the time had come, that under no circumstances could he wait too long and be captured. The next hour, when the news was good, he would postpone ending his life, grasping at the thought that by some miracle he might yet be successful in defeating the Russians, that the Allies might finally understand that their real enemy was Russia and help him drive the Soviets out of Germany. Each time that he wavered one way and then the other, Eva had to stand by and wait for his decision.

"If only it were finally over," she murmured to Frau Junge after one such incident. "I am so horribly worried about it."

On April 26 a diversion took Eva's mind off her fate for a few hours. Two young Waffen-SS orderlies, Grossman and Busse, decided that since it appeared they were going to die defending Berlin they would like to get married to their long-time girlfriends. The two women had joined the orderlies in the bunker. When the orderlies tried to see Hitler they were told that he was much too busy to talk with them. They contacted Eva, told her their problem and asked if she could obtain permission for them to marry in the bunker.

Eva nodded. "I will speak to the Führer. Wait here." Within a few minutes she was back. "The Führer is delighted to give his permission. If any of the parents are in Berlin and wish to attend the ceremony, the Führer will send an armored car for them."

Hitler and Eva both attended the double wedding that afternoon and afterwards extended their felicitations to the two young married couples. Erwin Jakubek, a waiter who also attended the ceremony, nudged Gerda Christian and pointed to Eva and the Führer. "They are deeply moved by the ceremony."

The secretary, flippant until the very end, grinned. "If Eva ever thought the Führer would marry her she knows better now. Time has run out."

She was wrong. Two days later, on April 28, Eva received a message from Grossmann, one of the orderlies who had been married in the bunker. She hurried to Hitler's study where the Führer was sitting and staring at the portrait of Frederick the Great. After kissing him on the cheek, Eva read Grossmann's note to him: "If I am killed in battle now I will die happy, because I was permitted to marry my sweetheart and the Führer congratulated me personally."

Hitler nodded but said nothing. However, when Eva held the note to her breast and murmured, "I am so happy for them," Hitler rose shakily from his chair and walked to her side. He had a message in his hand, too, but he didn't show it to Eva. Actually the message was tantamount to his death sentence, because it notified him that General Walther Wenck—upon whom he had depended to save Berlin—had been routed and his unit destroyed. Hitler leaned over and whispered into Eva's ear.

Frau Junge, who was at the other end of the room, saw Eva step back and stare at Hitler in amazement. He nodded, as though to reassure her, and then turned and went out the door calling for Goebbels. Eva, her eyes shining, walked over to Frau Junge and said, "Tonight you will certainly cry."

Frau Junge thought Eva meant she and Hitler were going to commit suicide that evening but she couldn't understand why Eva seemed so happy. Was she looking forward to dying? As Frau Junge went into the corridor she heard Goebbels issuing orders to several Waffen-SS soldiers to go to a certain Volkssturm detachment on the Friedrichstrasse and bring back Walter Wagner. At the time the name meant nothing to Frau Junge, but later she remembered that Wagner had married Goebbels years earlier.

During the remainder of the afternoon and early evening Eva stayed in her own quarters. This was unusual. Frau Junge and the others were accustomed to having her around, asking questions or trying to cheer everyone up when the news was bad. Eva's isolation further convinced the secretary that the end had come, that before the night was over both Eva and the Führer would be dead. Just before midnight Eva stepped from her room in Hitler's favorite dress, black silk with pink shoulder straps. She wore black suede shoes, a pearl necklace,

and a platinum watch with diamonds in place of numbers that Hitler had given her several years earlier. In her hair was a gold clip. She looked beautiful. Frau Junge leaned over to Gerda Christian and whispered, "Why is she dressed so well to die?"

A few minutes later Walter Wagner arrived. He was a justice of the peace who had been drafted to help defend Berlin. After Goebbels' messengers had located him and explained he was needed to perform a marriage ceremony, Wagner had gone to his home and picked up the necessary documents. It wasn't until he arrived in the bunker that he realized he had been summoned to marry the Führer and Eva Braun. He was so shocked to find himself in front of the Führer that he fumbled with the papers for several minutes. Finally Eva said, "Herr Wagner, can we get on with the ceremony? It is getting late."

Wagner nodded and placed the two-page marriage document on the small table near where he was standing. Asking the necessary questions one by one, he filled out the document in a methodical manner that made Eva more nervous than ever.

"Please hurry," she pleaded. Overhead she could hear the steady rumbling of the Russian artillery shells and the explosions of the Allied bombs. She had waited years for this wedding; she wanted it completed before it was too late.

Wagner was nervous, too. He didn't bother filling the blanks asking for the names of Hitler's father and mother, nor did he date the marriage license until after the ceremony. On the line asking for verification of Hitler's identity the harried justice of the peace scribbled, "Personally known." He did, however, take the time to ask Eva for her identity card, since he was not acquainted with her, and he filled in her birthplace and the names of her parents. Goebbels was a witness for Hitler and, ironically, Bormann stood beside Eva as her witness during the ceremony. To Eva's surprise, her most hated enemy seemed to enjoy the affair and was the first to congratulate her after the marriage. The four were asked to sign the document in the proper sequence at the end of the second page: Hitler, Eva, Goebbels and Bormann. Eva nearly signed "Braun" but corrected herself and wrote "Hitler." Then, as if an unseen witness was showering them with the traditional rice, a particularly close explosion above-ground shook flakes of white cement from the ceiling of the bunker onto Hitler and Eva.

The wedding party retired to Hitler's study for the Hochzeitsmahl (wedding breakfast). It was now nearly 2 A.M. on the morning of April 29, 1945. The two secretaries, Colonel von Below, Goebbels and his wife, Bormann and Fräulein Manzialy followed the elated Eva and the subdued Hitler into the room where champagne, wine and sweets were waiting. Hitler usually did not drink wine, but to celebrate his marriage he took a glass of sweet wine and joined in the toasts to his wife. After the others had finished offering their congratulations the Führer stood up at the end of the table and made a short speech. He recalled that he had been best man at Goebbels' wedding, and now Goebbels had repaid the debt by being his best man. He

paused a moment and then added that his wish had always been to return to his hometown in Austria and settle down with Eva to the life of an average citizen. He had hunted several times during the war for a place to build a home in the area, a place where he could spend the last years of his life in peace, but he had not found a suitable spot. Now, he said, it appeared that he would not need such a place.

To the small audience in the room the thought of the Führer leading the peaceful life of an ordinary citizen was incredible. They dismissed it as a fantasy induced by the sweet wine Hitler was drinking.

There was one minor irritation during the wedding party that bothered Eva. She couldn't understand why Hermann Fegelein, Gretl's husband, wasn't present. She remembered that she hadn't seen him for two days, and as Hitler continued reminiscing about the war and what he would have done had he been victorious, Eva slipped around the table to the chair next to Frau Junge. "Have you seen Fegelein?"

Frau Junge shook her head. She didn't know where he was, hadn't seen him for at least twenty-four hours.

Before Eva could question the secretary further, Hitler turned to Frau Junge and said, "Come, we must finish our work."

While Hitler had been waiting for

Eva talking to Bormann at the Berghof—he was seldom photographed in civilian clothes. It was no secret that Bormann and Eva hated each other; yet it was he who gave her away on her wedding night.

Wagner to arrive to marry him and Eva he had begun dictating his last will and testament to Frau Junge. Now he wanted to complete the task before it was too late. Eva returned to her own room to await Hitler, but shortly after putting on her negligee she received an urgent written message from her brother-in-law. "Eva, tell the Führer that I'm innocent. Beg him for a reprieve for me until I can prove my innocence. Please. I'm in the Reich Chancellery garden under guard."

Shocked, Eva immediately checked with Bormann in an effort to determine what kind of trouble Fegelein had become involved in that could be so serious. Bormann was delighted to tell her, confident that at last he could hurt her. Two nights ago, he said, Fegelein had slipped out of the bunker and had gone to his private house on the Kurfürstendamm. He had changed from his uniform to civilian clothes and was getting ready to escape from Berlin and go to the Berghof. From the Berghof, Bormann explained, Fegelein intended to go to Spain or Argentina. Hitler had noticed his absence, however, and sent several members of his bodyguard (under the command of Standartenführer Hoegl) to the Kurfürstendamm where they discovered Fegelein and brought him to the bunker.

"So?" Eva asked Bormann. "That is reason enough to shoot him?"

Bormann grinned. "A few hours ago Heinz Lorenz brought the Führer a Reuters report that stated Himmler was negotiating with Count Bernadotte to surrender Germany to the Allies. Your brother-in-law, as Himmler's liaison officer, undoubtedly was

in on the plot. It's too bad." Shaking with laughter, Bormann turned away.

Eva interrupted Hitler while he was still dictating his last will and testament, but it was useless. He ignored her plea to spare Fegelein because Gretl was expecting a child soon, despite the fact that Hitler had always liked Gretl.

"We can't allow family affairs to interfere with disciplinary action," Hitler snapped at his new wife. "Fegelein is a traitor just as Mussolini's son-in-law was a traitor, and you know what happened to him."

Eva recalled very clearly what had happened to Count Ciano. She also recalled that she had agreed with Hitler's decision to execute him. "Then you do plan to execute Hermann?"

Hitler nodded silently.

Eva returned to her own room and wrote a final message to Gretl's husband, who was waiting in the Reich Chancellery garden with the firing squad: "I can do nothing."

Within a matter of minutes Hermann Fegelein was shot to death near the same statue that Eva had asked Hitler to obtain for her private garden in Munich. Gretl was a pregnant widow at the age of thirty.

While Eva sobbed in her room, Hitler completed his dictation to Frau Junge, unconcerned over one more death sentence that he had pronounced. He was interested only in having his last will and testament in

A downcast Hitler: could he have read the writing on the wall?

proper form before the hour came to pronounce his own death sentence. In his private will he wrote:

Although during my years of struggle I believed I could not undertake the responsibility of marriage, I have now decided at the end of my life's journey to marry the young woman who, after many years of true friendship, came of her own free will to this city when it was almost completely under siege in order to share my fate. At her own desire she will go to her death with me as my wife. This will compensate us for what we both lost through my work in the service of my people.

What I possess belongs, insofar as it has any value at all, to the Party. Should this no longer exist, it belongs to the State, and should the State also be destroyed, any further decision from me is no longer necessary.

The paintings in the collections I bought over the years were never acquired for private purposes, but always exclusively for the establishment of an art gallery in my native town of Linz. It is my heartfelt desire that the legacy shall be fulfilled.

As executor of this document I appoint my most faithful party comrade Martin Bormann. He is authorized to make all decisions, which shall be legally binding. He is permitted to give everything of value either as mementos or such as is necessary for the maintenance of a petty bourgeois household to my brothers and sisters, and also above all to my wife's mother and to my faithful co-workers, male and female, who are all well known to him, principally my old secretaries, Frau Winter, etc., who have assisted me with their work over many years.

My wife and I choose death to avoid the disgrace of defeat or capitulation. It is our wish to be cremated immediately in the place where I have done the greatest part of my work during the course of my twelve years' service for my people.

It was four o'clock on the morning of April 29 when Hitler finished his last will and political testament and had them witnessed and signed by Bormann and the others. Eva, her eyes red from crying, was waiting when he reached their quarters. For the first time they went to bed together as man and wife. Their wedding night was punctuated by artillery explosions above the bunker.

Eva appeared in the corridor of the bunker shortly after 11 A.M., well groomed and happy. No one knew how to address her, and when the orderlies and adjutants stammered a greeting she smiled and said, "You can call me Frau Hitler if you wish."

She joined Hitler at the breakfast table and poured herself a cup of tea. Just as she was lifting the cup to her lips Linge, the valet, hurried across the room carrying a sheet of paper. Without a word he handed it to Hitler and walked away. Hitler read the message, so engrossed that he spilled his tea on his lap. Eva grabbed a towel and started to wipe the liquid from his clothing, but he just shook his head and handed her the sheet of paper. It was a Reuters dispatch that stated:

Benito Mussolini is dead. Captured by Italian partisans as he attempted to escape into Switzerland from northern Italy, he was taken before a tribunal and sentenced to death. In the village of Dongo the sentence was executed by partisans who machine-gunned him in the back. His mistress, Clara Petacci, who was with him at the time of the attempted escape, was also captured and also killed with the ex-Duce. Their bodies were taken to Milan and subjected to public degradation. After being dragged through the streets they were hung head downward in the public square where thousands spat at and reviled the corpses.

Hitler looked at Eva. "They will not do that to us. Our bodies will be burned."

Eva shuddered at his words and Frau Junge heard her mutter, "Don't say that. I don't want to think about it."

Hitler shrugged but said nothing. After drinking another cup of tea he started to rise from the breakfast table just as Dr. Ludwig Stumpfegger, the doctor who had replaced Brandt and Morell, walked into the room. Hitler called to him. "Would my dog Blondi respond to the cyanide the same as a human?"

"Yes, *mein Führer.*"

Hitler reached down and scratched Blondi, his inseparable companion for so many years. Giving her one final pat, he told Stumpfegger, "Take Blondi and give her a phial of the poison."

Eva watched until the dog disappeared down the corridor, then dropped her eyes to her plate. A few minutes later there was a loud barking, which soon faded to complete silence. Stumpfegger returned to the room and said, "The dog is dead."

Eva fingered her small phial and kept staring at the table. Hitler, however, asked the doctor if a man would still have the strength to pull the trigger of a revolver after he drank the poison. When Stumpfegger said that he would, Hitler looked at Eva. "We will take the poison and then use our pistols. That will make doubly certain that we will not be captured alive."

Eva, twisting her handkerchief into a knot, said, "Yes, yes, we will be certain."

Hitler then called a soldier to the breakfast table and gave him instructions to kill the five puppies that had been orphaned by Blondi's death. After making certain that the matter was taken care of, Hitler reread part of the testament Goebbels had written while he and Eva were asleep:

The Führer has ordered me, should the defense of the Reich capital collapse, to leave Berlin and to take part as a leading member in a government appointed by him. For the first time in my life I must categorically refuse to obey an order of the Führer. My wife and children join me in this refusal . . .

At that moment six small coffins were carried into the bunker, and Eva, knowing they were for the Goebbels' children, left the table and hurried from the room. As she stepped into the corridor, however, the children called to her and ran to her side. She kissed each one and continued on to her bedroom, recalling the many times she had sung them to sleep. Now they were scheduled for a sleep from which they would not awake.

For the remainder of that day, a Sunday, Hitler took care of the few remaining military and political matters in his collapsing Third Reich. He made certain that Admiral Karl Dönitz was appointed his successor; ordered Himmler's arrest; mandated that Göring remain a prisoner; and emphasized that Otto Skorzeny, the German commando leader who had rescued Mussolini earlier, should prepare a final defense against the Allies at the Alpine Redoubt south of Munich. While he was handling these matters, Eva went to bed. It was not until after 3 A.M. that Hitler joined her for their last night together.

Eva arose early, so early that she heard Otto Guensche ordering the jerricans full of gasoline to be placed near the bunker exit. She went directly to her own bedroom and called Frau Junge to join her. After the young secretary arrived, Eva opened her closet door, revealing the silver fox coat that she loved so much. "Frau Junge, I would like to give you this coat as a farewell gift."

Frau Junge thanked her but shook her head. "I don't think I will have need of it."

Eva approached the young secretary and embraced her. "Please try to get out. Perhaps you can still get through. If you do, greet Bavaria for me."

Frau Junge began to cry and left the room.

Hitler got up at noon and went directly to the conference room to check on the Russian advance. The news was all bad. Soviet guns were shelling the Reich Chancellery steadily, and Soviet troops were fighting in the underground tunnels at Friedrichstrasse. That meant that the enemy was within a block of the bunker. Hitler left the conference room immediately after studying the reports and summoned Hans Baur, his personal pilot, to the study. "Baur, I would like to take my leave of you."

The pilot, though he had been expecting the end, tried to talk the Führer out of killing himself. He offered to fly him to Argentina or Japan or Arabia, saying that he still thought he could pilot a plane out of Berlin. Eva, who had joined the two men in the study, watched Hitler eagerly, but when the Führer waved aside Baur's suggestion, her hopes faded.

"The war is over now that Berlin is finished," Hitler said, "and I stand or fall by the capital." He took the portrait of Frederick the Great down from the wall and handed it to Baur. "Take this with you. You deserve it." Hitler turned, grasped Eva's hand and said to her, "Now all I have is you."

Baur saw her smile and nod.

At 2:30 P.M. on April 30, Eva and Hitler had lunch with Frau Junge, Frau Christian and Fräulein Manzialy. As usual, Hitler ate no meat. Instead he had a small dish of spaghetti. Eva had tea, nothing else. The smell of gasoline had swept down through the bunker from the Reich Chancellery garden entrance, causing her to lose her appetite. She was aware that the gasoline was

Hitler with Blondi. In 1943, he said to Speer: "One of these days I'll have only two friends left—Fräulein Braun and my dog."

meant for her and Hitler. After they had finished eating Eva went back to her bedroom, Frau Christian to her quarters, Frau Junge to a small office across the corridor and Fräulein Manzialy to the kitchen to start preparations for the evening meal— even though it was obvious that Eva and Hitler would not be alive at the dinner hour.

At 3:30 P.M. Guensche announced throughout the bunker that the Führer wished to bid farewell to everyone and would be in the corridor within a few minutes. At approximately 3:45 P.M. Hitler, with Eva on his arm, appeared in the bunker corridor. Eva's hair was freshly washed and beautifully waved. She was wearing Hitler's favorite dress again and shoes she had bought in Italy. On her wrist was the platinum wristwatch studded with diamonds. While Hitler's face was solemn, Eva was smiling. Only the moisture in the corners of her eyes revealed her true feelings. She was calm, composed, quiet—and afraid.

Those who were left in the bunker bid the couple farewell, some with obvious relief that they were now free to try and escape, others in near panic. Frau Goebbels pleaded with Hitler not to kill himself, while her husband watched impassively. Goebbels had already decided that he, his

wife and children would die shortly after Hitler was pronounced dead. Frau Christian took this final opportunity to announce to Hitler that she intended to attempt an escape from the bunker. Hitler merely nodded.

Frau Junge quietly said, "Farewell."

Eva nodded and then kissed her. "Tell everyone in Munich farewell," she whispered. "Tell my parents I love them."

Then it was time to go. Hitler took Eva by the arm and together they entered the study. Just before the heavy iron door closed behind them, Eva looked back at Frau Junge and smiled.

It was a short wait for those outside the door. Within a few minutes a single pistol shot was heard—and then complete silence. When the door was opened, there was a heavy bitter-almond smell. Hitler was slumped on one end of the blue-and-white couch, blood running down his face from the single bullet he had fired from his Walther 7.65 pistol after swallowing the poison.

On the other end of the couch Eva was reclining as though asleep. Her little revolver was lying beside her, unfired, and beside it was her pink chiffon scarf. The empty phial that had contained the cyanide was on the floor near her feet. She was also dead—but she was still smiling.

Epilogue

After Eva and Hitler died and their bodies were burned in the Reich Chancellery garden, the others were left to decide their own fate. Frau Christian left the bunker in a group led by Otto Guensche to try and penetrate the Russian lines surrounding Berlin. A beauty with flawless complexion and near-perfect facial features, she would have been a prize catch for the women-starved Russian soldiers. After several narrow escapes on the way out, however, Frau Christian reached the American Zone safely. Today she lives in Dusseldorf.

Frau Junge donned men's clothing, slipped out of the bunker and mingled with the refugees fleeing Berlin. She reached Munich without being captured by the Russian troops and lives today in that city.

Fräulein Manzialy, the cook of whom Hitler had been so proud, wasn't so fortunate. She was last seen on the outskirts of Berlin being carried into a house by a Russian soldier while his comrades followed.

Fräulein Wolfe and Fräulein Schröder had departed Berlin before the death of Eva and Hitler and they survived the war. So did Hanna Reitsch, who piloted the last plane out of the capital. She resides in Frankfurt now. Eva's sister Gretl was at the Berghof when the fighting stopped and Ilse was in the Munich area as were Eva's parents. The two sisters live in the Munich area today but the parents have passed away.

Leni Riefenstahl survived the war to face a life of controversy because of her close association with Hitler. She, too, lives in Munich.

Albert Speer spent twenty years in prison after his conviction by the Allies as a war criminal. Today he divides his time between homes in Heidelberg and in the Allgäu mountains near the Swiss border.

Hans Baur, Hitler's personal pilot, flew out of Berlin on the day of Hitler's death. Otto Skorzeny, the Führer's top commando who rescued Mussolini, escaped from an Allied prison camp. Baur and Skorzeny were close friends during the post-war period and never wavered in their praise of Hitler.

They had each shared in the triumph of Hitler and, in the end, shared the tragedy of Hitler . . . as did Eva.

Index